Marion Landgraf

The Culturally
Deprived Child

The Culturally Deprived Child

by **FRANK RIESSMAN**

Chairman, Department of Psychology
BARD COLLEGE

HARPER & ROW, PUBLISHERS

New York, Evanston, and London

For

Cathy

contents

FOREWORD

American education today is beset by problems, and the most serious and significant among them is that which Professor Riessman has faced in this important book. Neglect of children from poor home backgrounds has been typical of most schools, both urban and rural. Pupils from culturally deprived homes are commonly resented as drawbacks to the morale and achievement of the school class. The fact that these youngsters do not see much value in formal academic routines, and have often been humiliated by failure, breeds in them hostility toward school authorities and, in a vicious circle, deepens the alienation between teachers and the very pupils who most need their help.

It has been one of the proud achievements of public education in the United States that we were the first country in the world to try to give education beyond the three R's to *all* our youths. Secondary education in other lands has been highly selective: the Lycées of France, the Grammar Schools of England, and the Gymnasia of Germany and Scandinavia have been designed for the intellectual upper crust only. Most Americans have rejected the aristocratic notion that a small circle of the elite from the "best homes" should have a virtual monopoly on higher education, and an access to top posts in government, business, and cultural life. We assert our dedication to the principle of equality of opportunity.

In recent decades a spate of anthropological, sociological, and social-psychological studies, many of them mentioned by Professor Riessman, has revealed the appalling gap between our pretensions and our practices. We do not give the same kind of food, clothing, housing, medical care, recreation, or justice to the deprived children that we give to those in comfortably-well-off homes. We don't like to think of class distinctions in American life, so we tend to shy away from these unacceptable facts. Opportunities are far from equal.

The American public school is a curious hybrid: it is managed by a school board drawn largely from upper-class circles; it is taught by teachers who come largely from middle-class backgrounds; and it is attended mainly by children from working-class homes. These three groups do not talk the same language. They differ in their manners, power, and hierarchies of values.

In the current flurry of concern over the "gifted," most well-to-do families are pleased to think of their own children as being given well-deserved special consideration. Teachers are gratified because "higher standards" are in vogue. Yet the great reservoir of undiscovered and undeveloped intellectual talent in America is not in upper-class or middle-class neighborhoods. While the proportion of high I.Q.'s may be lower in underprivileged areas —this is a slippery question, as Professor Riessman demonstrates— the actual numbers of intellectually very bright children in poor homes are far in excess of those to be found in the relatively few homes of business and professional leaders.

What is needed now is some fresh approach to the discovery and cultivation of the talents that undoubtedly exist among millions of children from unpromising backgrounds. The usual tests won't identify these able pupils; the usual curriculum won't challenge them; the usual teachers won't inspire them. While additional research would be helpful, the more urgent need seems to be for creative teaching on the basis of a different set of assumptions. It won't do to parade excuses, or to blame the individual, or the neighborhood. These pupils may not score high on verbal tests, but they are clever about many other things. They may be "uncooperative" in carrying out traditional assignments, but they often show extraordinary loyalty to their families or their gangs. Their parents may not volunteer for P.T.A. committees, but it would be wrong to assume that these parents are not concerned about what their children are able to achieve. Even their preference for television and movie shows over storybooks may arise from authentic awareness that print is actually a devious and impoverished medium in comparison with the presence of speaking, acting persons.

Under-cultured children have much to learn from education, but educators could well take some lessons from some of these youngsters. Their language may not be grammatical, but it is often more vivid and expressive than is the turgid prose of textbooks. These children face some of the "facts of life" more realistically than many of their teachers do. Even their pugnacity might be worth attention by some long-suffering, overworked, underpaid teachers. When it comes to making friends and standing by their pals, some children from underprivileged neighborhoods far outshine their priggish teachers.

The starting point is respect. Nothing else that we have to give will help very much if it is offered with a resentful, contemptuous, or patronizing attitude. We don't understand these neighborhoods, these homes, these children, because we haven't respected them enough to think them worthy of study and attention. Professor Riessman's book is likely to be the pioneer in a series of investigations that will reveal to America that we have neglected a major source of manpower and of creative talent. The stone which the builders rejected may even become the head of the corner.

Goodwin Watson
Teachers College
Columbia University

PREFACE

A number of the major problems facing us today require an understanding of the psychology of lower socio-economic, underprivileged groups. Psychiatrists have been notably unsuccessful with these individuals, as Hollingshead and Redlich document well. The understanding and treatment of juvenile delinquents from disadvantaged backgrounds has been something less than earthshaking, and the cleavage between the deprived child and the school appears to have reached new heights.

It is to this last problem that the present book is primarily addressed. But the book is intended also for all social practitioners who are concerned with underprivileged groups.

In short, the aim is to provide teachers, social workers, psychologists, and psychiatrists with a picture of the deprived individual, including his psychology and his culture, that will enable them to work with this individual in a fruitful, nonpatronizing manner. The book attempts to develop new approaches to underprivileged individuals by emphasizing the positive aspects of their cultures which, hitherto, have been largely ignored.

Most current approaches emphasize the need for more and better teachers, smaller classes, and the like. Who could disagree? But we should like to show how an understanding of the psychology of the deprived can perhaps produce much greater academic success than is presently envisioned. The difference between our orientation and existing views is highlighted in Chapter XI, which offers a critical evaluation of the Higher Horizons Program—undoubtedly the best contemporary project aimed at educating deprived children.

The sources for the book are as follows: my own experience with lower socio-economic groups as a researcher and participant-observer (reported in *Journal of Social Issues*, Winter, 1949). Included also under the heading of experience are the many years of teaching and working with the teachers of underprivileged youngsters. Apart from my own special research investigations (see Bibliography), I have attempted to integrate the extensive literature on lower socio-economic groups, in order to establish a framework for comprehending the psychology of these individuals.

The works of the following investigators are especially pertinent: Bennett Berger, Urie Bronfenbrenner, Ely Chinoy, Allison Davis, Ernest Haggard, August Hollingshead, Seymour Lipset, Eleanor Maccoby, Hyman Rodman. Special attention is given to two recent books: *Inner Conflict and Defense*, by Daniel Miller and Guy Swanson, and *Education and Income*, by Patricia Sexton. In addition to the published research of these writers, I have been fortunate in having access to unpublished findings of what is probably the most extensive investigation of educational problems of deprived children. This investigation, currently in progress, is being conducted under the auspices of the Institute For Developmental Studies of the Department of Psychiatry at New York Medical College. The co-director of this study, Martin Deutsch, has kindly made available much of the rich research material emanating from this study.

I would like to acknowledge the special assistance of the following people: S. M. Miller, with whom I have worked jointly for a number of years in formulating many of the concepts utilized in the present book; Catherine Riessman, for special help in formulating and presenting some of the central ideas of the book; Walter Murray, for permitting me to quote his unpublished paper on "Assumptions Underlying the Intelligence Test"; Patricia Sexton, for permitting me to see the galley proofs of her book, *Education and Income*, in advance of publication; Irving Taylor, for his assistance in clarifying the creative potential of deprived children; Vernon Halprecht for his help in explaining the Hunter College Program directed toward preparing teachers for schools in underpriviliged areas; Shelly Koenigsberg, for many valuable insights concerning the teaching of deprived children; Helen Davidson, for her encouragement and stimulation; and Bard College, for a special research grant.

Special thanks are also due to: George Bereday, Lawrence

Cremin, Miriam Goldberg, David Hunter, Harold Kirsch, Judith Krugman, Sol Levine, Edna Meyers, Frank Oja, Winston Robbins, Henry Saltzman, Jerome Siller, Mae Stern, and to Viking Press for permitting me to quote from *Education and Income* by Patricia Sexton.

The Culturally
Deprived Child

i

ONE IN THREE

In 1950, approximately one child out of every ten in the fourteen largest cities of the United States was "culturally deprived."[1] *By 1960, this figure had risen to one in three.* This ever increasing trend is due to their rapid migration to urban centers. By 1970, it is estimated there may be one deprived child for every two enrolled in schools in these large cities.

When one considers that almost one-sixth of the population of the entire nation resides in these cities; that between 1940 and 1950 eighty per cent of the national growth in population occurred in metropolitan areas; and that between 1950 and 1957 ninety-seven per cent of the national growth occurred in these same areas, the dimensions and urgency of the problem are readily apparent.[2]

Clearly one of the most pressing problems facing the urban school today is the "culturally deprived child."

[1] The terms "culturally deprived," "educationally deprived," "deprived," "underprivileged," "disadvantaged," "lower class," "lower socio-economic group," are used interchangeably throughout this book.
[2] The Great Cities School Improvement Studies," Ford Foundation Project, mimeographed, 1960.

Why Educate the Deprived Child?

The purpose of this book is to challenge the widely-held notion that the "culturally deprived" child is not interested in education, and to present a new "cultural" approach for teaching these children.

Why is education of this disadvantaged group so important? It would be easy to answer that we must educate the deprived because they are a source of needed manpower, or because everyone deserves an education. But perhaps there is a deeper reason. It is essential to democracy to combat the anti-intellectualism, prejudice, and intolerance that are bound to be characteristic of any educationally deprived group, and are, in fact, dominant motifs of the disadvantaged in America. Fundamentally, education combats narrow thinking. The groups who lack education have contributed disproportionately to discrimination, bigotry, and attacks on freedom of thought. Education is not merely something that we would like all groups to receive for their own good; it is as vitally necessary to us, the educators, as it is to the uneducated.

There is another reason why a meaningful approach to the deprived is important to the educator. Most teachers who work with underprivileged children today find this a most unattractive, unrewarding task. It can be both a challenging and an interesting assignment if a different approach is used.

What is needed is a sympathetic, noncondescending, understanding of the culture of the underprivileged. We need to comprehend the deprived person's attitudes toward education, the school, and the teacher. Many of his attitudes toward education are more positive than we might think, although his attitudes toward the school and the teacher may be negative. This contradiction between education and the school must be resolved.

We will endeavor to show why the deprived individual, although desiring education, is antagonistic toward the school. Although we recognize that both the school and the parents are at fault in producing the existing educational problems, we wish to emphasize the need for corrective action in the school—for it is there that we are more likely to produce large-scale changes than in the home, which we can influence but little.

While there may be aspects of the culture of the deprived individual that would be better changed, it is necessary for the educator to work within the framework of the culture as it exists. In other words, the culture should be accepted as given. There is one fundamental exception to this principle—one area in which the educator avowedly attempts to oppose the culture of the underprivileged, and that is with regard to anti-intellectualism and narrow pragmatism. While we may understand the reasons for the anti-intellectualism, we are not required to be uncritical of it.

Culturally Deprived or Educationally Deprived?

A word is necessary about the term "culturally deprived." While lower socio-economic groups lack many of the advantages (and disadvantages) of middle-class culture, we do not think it is appropriate to describe them as "culturally deprived." As we shall see, they possess a culture of their own, with many positive characteristics that have developed out of coping with a difficult environment. The term "culturally deprived" refers to those aspects of middle-class culture—such as education, books, formal language—from which these groups have not benefited. However, because it is the term in current usage, we will use "culturally deprived" interchangeably with "educationally deprived" to refer to the members of lower socio-economic groups who have had limited access to education.

Who Are the Deprived?

Paul Goodman points out that "In our economy of abundance it is still subject to discussion whether or not there is as much poverty as there was in the Thirties when 'one third of a nation was ill-housed, ill-clothed, ill-fed.' Some say 20 per cent are poverty-stricken, some as many as 40 per cent. Census, 1958: 31 per cent."[3]

A large portion of the current disadvantaged population is composed of cultural and racial minorities.

When we think of the deprived sub-culture, we do not take as our model that segment which is most disorganized by the en-

[3] Paul Goodman, *Growing Up Absurd* (New York: Random House, 1960), p. 52.

vironment. This group, despite the disproportionate public attention it receives, is surprisingly small. We do not think that much can be learned about how to educate the mass of the underprivileged from examining this small element. On the contrary, from investigating the main disadvantaged groups and their cultures, we may gain insights that are valuable in dealing with the disorganized minority.

A quotation from Robert Weaver, the new Housing Administrator, is useful in characterizing the mainstream of the deprived:

> Slums in American cities today house families which hold a wide range of values and evidence a variety of behavior patterns. Some are households with female heads and are stable none-the-less; others may be ungrammatical but adhere to high moral standards; still others evidence all the attributes of middle-class behavior and are dedicated to its values, if not recipients of its rewards. All three groups have ambition and talent, but fight an uphill battle in maintaining respectability and achievement for themselves and their children. . . .[4]

Weaver also characterizes the disorganized minority element in the following way:

> Certain elements now concentrated in the slums, however, present clear well-defined problems; they include the confirmed middle-aged winos, the established prostitutes, the overt homosexuals, the hardened criminals, and the like, who either resist rehabilitation, or require long-term assistance of a most intensive type. They are multi-ethnic and constitute the real "hard core."[5]

The main groups in the underprivileged communities strongly dislike this anarchic, criminal element, and thus represent important allies for the social practitioners.

Why Johnny Can't Learn

Countless reasons are offered to explain why underprivileged children do poorly in school. Here is a partial list of the conventional reasons:

1. The lack of an "educational tradition" in the home, few books, etc.

[4] "Human Values of Urban Life," *Proceedings of the Academy of Political Science*, May, 1960, pp. 33–34.
[5] *Ibid.*, p. 34.

2. Insufficient language and reading skills.

3. Inadequate motivation to pursue a long-range educational career, and poor estimate of self.

4. Antagonism toward the school, the teacher.

5. Poor health, improper diet, frequent moving, and noisy, TV-ridden homes.

Undoubtedly there is much truth in this listing and we will attempt to illuminate some of these factors and what may be done about them. But implicit in this list is the emphasis on the non-school environment, the parents, and the child himself, as the central determinants of the failure to learn. What has happened to the old idea that held if the children aren't learning, look to the teacher? Scant attention is given to the faults of the school in the present-day analysis of the problem. It is almost as though the school were saying: "We want to teach these kids—we try very hard—but they don't want to learn because their parents and friends don't want them to."

By refocusing on the school's contribution, we think we may be able to make suggestions on which the school can take direct action, rather than blaming a home environment over which the school has little power. Furthermore, some of the conventional causes given for Johnny's failure to learn may now be recast in a new light. For example, instead of talking about poor motivation and antagonism toward the school, reference will be made to the rejecting attitudes of the teacher toward Johnny, and the resulting anger and loss of interest on the part of the child.

Let us then try to reformulate some basic factors deterring Johnny from learning, with which we shall be concerned in this book:

1. The discrimination, frequently unintentional, seen in the classroom, Parent-Teacher Association, guidance office, psychological testing program, etc., which alienates Johnny and his family.

2. Johnny's *ambivalence* toward education—not simply rejection of it—his lack of school know-how, test-taking skills, information concerning college, and his anti-intellectualism.

3. The culture of the school which overlooks and under-estimates his particular skills and mode of intellectual functioning that arise out of his culture and way of life.

4. The deficits in Johnny's background which necessitate special *transitional* techniques to bring him into the academic mainstream. These do not require a "soft" approach, a lowering of standards, a capitulation to his deficiencies.

A Cultural Approach: Culture vs. Environment

It is easy to say that we must understand the culture of the underprivileged. Most people would agree. The question is, what do we mean by a cultural approach? Some people seem to think that the culture of a group is equivalent to its environment. Therefore, the culture of lower socio-economic groups is seen to include inadequate housing, limited access to leisure facilities, and the like. We prefer to distinguish between the environment, or conditions of life, of a group, and the culture of that group. We conceive the latter to be the methods that have evolved for coping with the conditions of life. Thus, "culture" would include the traditions, values, and mores of a specific group, many of which have a long history. Values and attitudes of the underprivileged that are relevant for the educator would include beliefs about punishment, authority, games, cooperation, competition, introspection, intellectuals, etc.

Along with customs and traditions, culture consists of the institutions, the structures, and the methods of organization of the people involved. The storefront church and the protest movement, the trade union and the fraternal lodge, the large extended family, the neighborhood club or gang, are illustrative here.

Thus, we view culture as an effort to cope with the surrounding environment. Many of the coping techniques are ineffective or devious, of course, but we believe that only if they are seen in terms of an effort to grapple with the milieu will they be properly understood. If we fail to see the struggle, the attempts to combat the difficult environment, and instead seize upon the failures, the ineffectiveness, we will not understand the behavior of the educationally deprived or, at best, will see it only one-sidedly.

Imitation and Rebellion: Two Sides of the Same Coin

An important question that arises here concerns the formation of this culture. It is easy to believe that the underprivileged, surrounded as they are by television, movies, and the other mass media, simply mimic the dominant mores of the society. Carrying the process one step further, it is often contended that minority members incorporate the dominant group's views of them; therefore, they have low self-esteem and sometimes self-hatred. Undoubtedly there is some truth to these assertions; the underprivileged are unquestionably affected by the mass communications system and the images of the deprived presented therein. But culture is not primarily determined by words and symbols, but by people. Perhaps the culture of the deprived is not decisively produced by the mass media, but rather by the interactions of disadvantaged groups and individuals with each other, over a long period of time.

Alongside the view that the deprived person's culture is largely reflective of the mainstream culture, an apparently opposite thesis has emerged. Here the culture of the deprived is seen as a contra-culture, in which the characteristic feature is rebellion and opposition to the dominant way of life. This culture is supposed to be typical of many delinquent gangs. Again, there is a measure of truth in this view—the culture of the disadvantaged does have certain rebellious, angry features, and certainly some of the sub-cultures within the deprived society could be most aptly characterized in this fashion. But again, the implicit, somewhat ethnocentric, belief seems to hold that underprivileged culture is fundamentally determined by the dominant society—this time not as a simple mirroring, but in direct opposition. It is as though we were saying "These people have no way of shaping their own lives other than by trying to do what we do or by doing just the opposite—they can't think for themselves and find their own paths."

The Value of the Cultural Approach for the Teacher

There are two ways in which a cultural approach can aid the educator. One has to do with the social-emotional relationship between the teacher and the educationally deprived child; the other is more directly concerned with the way subject matter can best be taught.

A sound cultural understanding should enable the teacher to establish a much better relationship with the deprived child who is typically antagonistic toward the school and, on the surface at least, unmotivated to learn. Through an empathic understanding of his culture, the teacher will begin to see why the deprived child is hostile, what he expects of her, why he wants her to prove herself. The teacher will come to learn why he needs a structured classroom, how she can utilize his in-group loyalty, informality, equalitarianism, humor, and the like. She will come to understand why he does not need "love" but respect. And finally, she will be able to interpret in a new light much of the behavior which appears negative. What previously appeared to be emotional imbalance and supersensitivity to minor frustrations can now be seen anew.

An interesting illustration of how knowledge of the culture of the underprivileged can be useful, not only to the teacher, but to other social practitioners as well, can be seen in regard to low-income public housing. Often politically minded people are astonished at the lack of interest which disadvantaged groups manifest toward the public housing movement. Believing that these projects are essentially valuable for lower socio-economic groups, they cannot comprehend the resistance frequently encountered.

Only when it is realized that the rules governing admission into public housing violate the traditions and mores of the deprived culture does this resistance become comprehensible. In order to obtain an apartment in a public housing project, it is necessary to have a standard family unit of father, mother, and children. Grandparents, aunts, uncles, and other relatives, with whom the deprived family may have been sharing an apartment, are not accepted as part of the basic family unit.[6] The extended family pattern, which is an important part of the culture of the deprived and plays a major communal role in their lives, is thus ignored. It is no wonder then that they have misgivings about public housing. Also, the housing administrations will not accept families in which the parents are unmarried. Furthermore, projects are constructed in so-called "slum neighborhoods," and the large numbers of people in these areas who do not qualify for public housing are swept back ("relocated") into other areas, which are

[6] Recently some emendations have been made in the Public Housing law providing for exceptions to this principle.

further overcrowded. The communal ties which existed in the original neighborhood are thereby destroyed.

To sum up: effective education of the "one in three" who is deprived requires a basic, positive understanding of his traditions and attitudes. One of the most important attitudes to understand is that of the disadvantaged toward education itself. We turn to this problem in the next chapter.

ii

ARE THE CULTURALLY DEPRIVED INTERESTED IN EDUCATION?

It is popularly held that the culturally deprived child is not interested in education; moreover, that he is essentially antagonistic toward it. This idea is rooted in two obvious facts: one is the observation that he is plainly discontented in the school; the other is the equally well-known fact that his parents have little education, frequently cannot read, and that there are typically few, if any, books in his home.

In light of these observations, we were interested to come upon a finding which indicated that members of underprivileged groups had a rather surprising view about the importance of education.[1] Interviewees were asked the question, "What do you miss most in life that you would like your children to have?" Over 50 per cent of the white lower socio-economic group (and 70 per cent of the Negro group) said "education." Even more significant is the fact that the respondents supplied the word "education"; they did not select it from a list of possible choices provided by the interviewer. This would seem to mean that education, at some level, not only is important to this group, but also is in the forefront of their minds.

This is not an isolated finding. Sears and Maccoby in their study of *Patterns of Child Rearing* found that deprived parents

[1] Frank Riessman, *Workers' Attitudes Towards Participation and Leadership,* unpublished Ph.D. dissertation, Columbia University, 1955.

are more concerned that their children do well in elementary school than are middle-class parents.[2] This, of course, may be due, in part, to the fact that middle-class children are doing fairly well in the first place and so require less attention. But it also indicates a degree of interest in education on the part of the culturally deprived parent.

It is generally believed that deprived children receive little educational help in their homes. Yet, in a recent study, Professor Dolores Durkin reported that *over 55 per cent of the children who had learned to read before coming to school came from lower socio-economic homes.*[3] "... family interviews consistently revealed a ready, even enthusiastic, acceptance of pre-school reading ability on the part of the lower-class families; and, to the contrary, something of a guilt feeling reaction from the higher classes. It could be hypothesized, certainly, that this difference in attitude at least partially accounted for the social-class distribution found for the subjects in this study." Professor Durkin indicates that it is apparently the older brother or sister who plays the decisive role in helping the child to read before he comes to school.

Another relevant fact is the attitude toward college education. When compared with higher socio-economic groups, the underprivileged are less interested in college for their children. But there is a substantial percentage that feels that college is a necessity. Near the end of World War II, the following question was asked on a nationwide poll: "After the war, if you had a son (daughter) graduating from high school, would you prefer that he (she) go on to college, or would you rather have him (her) do something else, or wouldn't you care one way or the other?" Sixty-eight per cent of the "poor" (in contrast to 91 per cent of the "prosperous") responded affirmatively to the college choice.[4] (It is perhaps most striking that the women were more

[2] Robert R. Sears, Eleanor E. Maccoby, and Harry Levin, *Patterns of Child Rearing* (Evanston: Row, Peterson & Company, 1957), p. 430.

[3] Dolores Durkin, "Children Who Learn to Read Prior to First Grade: A Second-Year Report." Paper presented at American Educational Research Association Meeting, Chicago, February, 1961.

[4] Reported by Herbert H. Hyman, "The Value Systems of Different Classes: A Social Psychological Contribution to the Analysis of Stratification," in *Class, Status, and Power* by Reinhard Bendix and Seymour Martin Lipsit (Glencoe: The Free Press, 1953), pp. 430–431.

positive about this than the men. Since the women are likely to be more influential in child rearing, one might venture to say that their preference for a college education has more weight.)

When young people themselves were asked a similar question, between 40 and 50 per cent emphasized the need for a college education.[5]

It is clear then that a substantial proportion of the under-privileged group is interested in higher education. This aspiration, of course, may be tempered considerably by the actual economic possibilities. But this works both ways because the individual who does not indicate a desire for a college education may be suppressing this desire because he feels it is economically unfeasible. Mulligan found among the sons of blue-collar workers a marked increase of interest in education as a result of the educational opportunities afforded by the G.I. Bill.[6]

Further evidence that the culturally deprived have a greater interest in education than a superficial appraisal might indicate is found in the success of the Demonstration Guidance Project and the Higher Horizons Program in New York City. Apart from the achievements of this Program with regard to improvement in academic performance and intelligence test scores, the enormous increase in interest is shown by the higher rate of attendance and improved discipline of the children, and the participation of the parents at P.T.A. meetings. (This Program will be discussed more fully in Chapter XI.)

The Meaning of Education

What does education mean to the culturally deprived? It is perhaps easier to state what it does not mean. First, it does not have the same meaning that it has for many middle-class Americans. There is practically no interest in knowledge for its own sake; quite the contrary, a pragmatic anti-intellectualism prevails. Nor is education seen as an opportunity for the development of self-expression, self-realization, growth, and the like; consequently, progressive approaches are opposed.

There are varied motives for education among the deprived,

[5] *Ibid.*, p. 432.
[6] Raymond A. Mulligan, "Socio-Economic Background and College Enrollment," *American Sociological Review*, April, 1951, p. 196.

some more apparent than others. The utilitarian attitudes are easiest to grasp. The average deprived person is interested in education in terms of how useful and practical it can be to him. Education provides the means for more and different kinds of employment, provides a more secure future. Jobs that interest him, like fireman, policeman, postal clerk, all require fairly detailed civil service examinations, and education is sorely needed to obtain these coveted positions.

The underprivileged person is much more oriented to the vocational, in contrast to the academic aspect of education. What is possibly less well known is that education serves purposes other than job improvement. One respondent told us, "I want education so that I can handle the red tape you run into all over nowadays. If you want to buy a TV on time, or get a driver's license, you've got to fill out papers and be able to read; the same thing for a lot of jobs, the unemployment check, getting an apartment in public housing, signing a lease." In short, he wants education in order to deal with the bureaucracy which he feels surrounds him. Education is desired to enable him to cope better with the everyday problems of a complex society.

A respondent who came from a deprived background, but is now a college student, put it differently: "Without some education the world is a vague blur. Words are powerful and without them you don't understand what's going on, you can't say what you want or feel. People can fool you easily and they look down on you. Education gives you pride."

Another reason why the deprived individual wants education relates to his great respect for physical science. This respect is based on a number of different factors. One is the fact that he has a much more physical, non-symbolic approach to life that has its beginnings in his childhood experiences. Another source of the respect for science appears to be the feeling that through knowledge of science and machines comes mastery and control over the complex world. The deprived individual feels powerless in most spheres of life, and he sees science as giving him control and strength, at least over the outer world. A third, more obvious, reason is because he sees a career in this area much more readily. The kind of work he has done all his life seems a lot nearer to mechanics and science than it does to any of the other academic disciplines.

From his attitudes toward education it is not at all difficult to predict which subjects he will like in school. His interests center around the three R's and the sciences, while he is least interested in social studies, literature, and the arts, as they are now presented in the school. One might expect, however, that in light of his pragmatic, non-abstract, orientation he would prefer the approach of progressive education with its emphasis on learning by doing. In order to understand why this is not so, why, on the contrary, he is most antagonistic to progressive methods, it will be necessary to consider his traditionalism, with emphasis on his attitude toward discipline, structure, and authority. (We turn to this question in Chapter IV.)

Education vs. the School

But now we return to our fundamental problem. If the deprived individual is, in fact, interested in education for the reasons we have noted, why is it that he encounters such difficulty in the school?

There are at least three reasons, two of which relate to attitudes and practices of the school, and the third, which concerns the conflicting feelings of the underprivileged individual himself.

Although the deprived person in many ways desires education, he is inhibited by a number of significant factors. For one thing, he does not think he has a good chance of getting much education. This feeling forces his educational aspirations to remain more at the wish or fantasy level, rather than making of them a definite concrete intention. Then, the mechanics of obtaining higher education are quite vague to him. Getting admitted to college, no less attending classes, is complicated and foreign. He feels threatened by the red tape and his general lack of information concerning the procedures involved. He does not know what he is supposed to say in an interview, or to answer on an application blank in response to the question: "Why do you want to go to college —what do you expect to get out of college?"

Most of his friends and relatives do not go to college and he fears he will be out of place. Even more serious, he fears the loss of his familial, community, and peer group ties.

Apart from these limiting factors that are more internal to him, there is the fact that education has a different meaning to the culturally deprived individual than it does to the educator. The teacher, and most non-deprived students, consider knowledge for its own sake important. It does not have to be useful. Knowledge alone is power, and abstract symbolism need have no practical application. This view of learning is the antithesis of the deprived view. Moreover, self-expression and self-actualization, other aims of education, particularly modern education, are equally alien to the more pragmatic, traditional, underprivileged person. These differences alone might be sufficient to produce a negative attitude toward the school. But this is only part of the story. The school has developed, often unconsciously, various forms of subtle, but pervasive, discrimination against disadvantaged children. We will discuss these in the next chapter.

Our thesis is that this discrimination has produced the alienation and anger against the school system that are found in these children and their parents. Their dislike of the school is often confused with antagonism toward education.

Summary

Education is desired by the culturally deprived more than is generally recognized. Different segments probably want education for different reasons. Some desire it for vocational improvement, others so that they will not be deceived as easily in the modern world, still others because of their respect for science. The difficulty in the school system arises because the school stresses education for its own sake and as a means for the development of self-expression—orientations which the culturally deprived do not share. Furthermore, the discrimination unwittingly practiced in the school aggravates the problems, and produces the schism between school and education.

iii

DISCRIMINATION WITHOUT
PREJUDICE

Not long ago a friend said: "Why bother showing that discrimination exists in the schools; everyone knows that the average middle-class teacher is going to have a different point of view from the disadvantaged child, and some prejudice is bound to crop up."

There are two fundamental reasons why it is necessary to discuss discrimination:

1. Its pervasiveness and subtety in the school system are far greater than is imagined, and it is *unwittingly* practiced even by the best-intentioned people. As we shall see, discrimination can function without prejudice.

2. By stressing that discrimination against the underprivileged child by his teacher is one of the important reasons why "Johnny can't learn," we shift some of the blame from his environment, family, and motivation onto ourselves. This may constrain against patronization and permit us to understand, and be more sympathetic toward, Johnny's anger and resentment.

When we complain about the waste of talent resulting from the non-education of the underprivileged child, it is easier to blame his "defeatist feelings," or "poor educational tradition," than to place an important share of the responsibility on ourselves. Yet, the educator has more potential control over his own behavior, his own prejudices, than he does over the various aspects of

Johnny's environment that he believes to be the prime causes of the deprived child's academic difficulties.

Discrimination: Overt and Subtle

Some of the traditional forms of discrimination no longer characteristically exist. For example, many people claim that the school buildings in underprivileged neighborhoods are poorer, that these schools have less equipment, fewer teachers, and so on. Ten or fifteen years ago this was largely true, but in the last decade, at least in many of the large metropolitan areas, the trend has been to reverse this pattern. Thus, in New York City many new school buildings have appeared in deprived communities and frequently these schools are given excellent equipment.[1] The problem is more complex, however, because even though these well equipped schools are being built, and the standard teacher-student ratio prevails in disadvantaged neighborhoods, nevertheless the *teacher turnover is far greater in these areas.* Teachers much prefer to teach "nice" children in "nice" schools, in "nice" zones. Principals continually report that it is difficult to keep good teachers in the schools in the poorer areas of the city. Teachers, especially women, are often afraid to teach in these schools, and in general find the task less stimulating, less rewarding. Thus, new buildings do not remove discrimination.

There is no need to document at length the various overt forms of discrimination, but a brief listing is necessary in order to give some feeling for the pervasiveness of the problem: the reading texts used in the classrooms which typically contain material far less attuned to the interests of the disadvantaged; the Parent-Teacher Associations which often patronize or ignore underprivileged parents; the intelligence tests, the applicability of which to lower socio-economic groups is increasingly being questioned; the school psychologists and guidance counselors, who frequently underestimate the possibility of the economically underprivileged child going to college; the friendship cliques and clubs which favor less the child from a poor neighborhood; the teacher's un-

---

[1] Sexton notes, however, that in "Big City" (the large Midwestern city she surveyed), underprivileged neighborhoods still have the oldest school buildings, poorest facilities, etc. See Patricia Sexton, *Education and Income* (New York: The Viking Press, Inc., 1961), pp. 122-134.

favorable images and expectations which militate against the respect and encouragement so needed by the child.[2]

Lest it be believed that teachers react primarily to the academic inadequacies of disadvantaged children, rather than their values, we report a recent study by Davidson and Lang. They found that teachers were less favorably inclined toward deprived children *even when their school achievements were good*. Furthermore, they observed that the underprivileged children accurately perceived the teachers' rejection of them. Davidson and Lang also found that the teachers' negative image of the deprived child is reflected in a lowering of the child's self-perception or self-image, as well as affecting his academic achievement and classroom behavior.[3]

It is often contended that one of the main reasons disadvantaged children are not admitted to college is because of their relatively low I.Q. scores.

Sibley points out that the differential in college admissions is not primarily due to intelligence, but rather to economic status. With an intelligence quotient of over 110, the deprived high school student has much less chance of going to college than the middle-class student with the same I.Q. In fact, over 60 per cent of the underprivileged individuals with I.Q.'s of better than 110 never get to college.[4]

It is necessary to clarify at this point that the I.Q. referred to is obtained on the standard intelligence tests which, as we point out elsewhere in this book, are strongly biased in favor of the nondeprived child.

Harvard University has been especially concerned about this problem. In a critical report, a special committee on admissions policy warned that Harvard receives few students from lower income groups and almost none from the lowest. Dean Munro

---

[2] For a more extensive discussion see Patricia Sexton, *Education and Income* (New York: The Viking Press, Inc., 1961), especially chapters II, IV, V.

[3] Helen H. Davidson and Gerhard Lang, "Children's Perception of Their Teachers' Feelings Toward Them Related to Self-Perception, School Achievement and Behavior," *Journal of Experimental Education*, December, 1960, pp. 107–118.

[4] Elbridge Sibley, "Some Demographic Clues to Stratification" in *Sociological Analysis*, edited by Logan Wilson and William L. Kolb (New York: Harcourt, Brace & Company, 1949), pp. 646–649.

thinks that "professors should haunt 'submerged' schools with the same tenacity as football coaches. . . . Why should 300 college representatives visit New Trier High School each year, and barely any, except coaches, visit the big downtown Chicago high school, only 20 miles away?"[5]

Of course, educational discrimination operates long before the individual reaches the high school level.

Hollingshead points out that deprived children are the least popular in school; they are less often permitted into the major cliques; they are more often perceived as unattractive, etc.[6]

The Hidden Dissuaders[7]

We now present three forms of discrimination which manifest varying degrees of sublety and unawareness on the part of their perpetrators. First, we survey some new dimensions in school segregation, then take a look at a complex form of discrimination emanating from the guidance office, and finally present a brief exposition of the manifestations and causes of patronization.

The pattern of segregation found in our northern cities is more subtle, and sometimes more unintentional, than the conspicuous racial segregation of the South. Bruno Bettelheim states the issue in an illuminating article, aptly subtitled "Should the Gifted Be Educated Separately?"[8] The South, says Bettelheim, seems to be moving "ever so reluctantly . . . from 'separate but equal' toward integration; while the white, liberal, middle-class North seems to be aiming (not in principle, but in actual practice) at school arrangements which can best be described as separate and unequal."[9] In analyzing the pattern of Northern segregation, Bettelheim states:

> Here, the separation of the 'nice' white children from the poor
> white and Negro children is accomplished both by the enlarge-

[5] *Time Magazine*, November 21, 1960, p. 56.

[6] August B. Hollingshead, *Elmtown's Youth* (New York: John Wiley & Sons, Inc., 1950), Chapter IX.

[7] We are indebted to President Mary Bunting of Radcliffe College for the term "hidden dissuaders," which she uses to describe the various institutions that subtly dissuade women from pursuing intellectual work (the *New York Times*, November 27, 1961, News of the Week in Review, p. 7).

[8] Bruno Bettelheim, "Sputnik and Segregation," *Commentary*, October, 1958, pp. 332–339.

[9] *Ibid.*, p. 332.

ment of the private and parochial school systems, and by the move to the suburbs—a move for which the family's main reasons are usually the better suburban schools and the fact that the children will associate with more desirable playmates than would be the case in the city. In the white suburbs the children are supposed to enjoy better cultural opportunities. These opportunities, strangely enough, are no longer equated with being close to the cultural facilities that an urban center offers, but rather with lawns and trees, though historically cultural advances have been tied to urban and not rural life.[10]

Bettelheim notes that the "liberal" seems to be fighting "for equal opportunities for the rest of the population, plus special opportunities for our own group, the intelligentsia. Or, closer to fact, the special educational privileges of white over Negro should be eliminated, but special educational opportunities should be created for the intellectual elite."[11] The old "white color" elite is to be replaced by a "white-collar" elite.

The desire for special education for the gifted does not, of course, reflect any direct *prejudice* against the disadvantaged. It only functions as an indirect, but powerful lever of *discrimination*.

Segregation affects underprivileged children in countless ways, but perhaps most disturbing is the effect on their long-range educational aspirations. Deprived children attending "integrated" schools where there are large numbers of middle-class children are much more likely to want to go to college and embark upon professional careers, according to a recent study of the San Francisco–Oakland Bay Area in California.[12]

Of course, much segregation is not produced within the school itself, but reflects the residential pattern. The higher incomes of the middle-class individuals tend to produce considerable residential segregation. In some communities, for example, there has been a history of enforced income and job segregation. In Aliquippa, Pennsylvania, the home of Jones and Laughlin Steel, the town was laid out in a series of zones, each restricted to particular kinds of office and factory workers. In Massena, New York, where Alcoa was the chief source of employment, a more informal scheme led

[10] *Ibid.*, p. 332.
[11] *Ibid.*, p. 333.
[12] Allen B. Wilson, "Class Segregation and Aspirations of Youth," *American Sociological Review*, December, 1959, pp. 836–845.

to somewhat similar results. While these were one-company towns with special histories, similar residential segregation has taken place in most large cities.

Love Is Not Enough

Some years ago, a leader of the Urban League informed us of a pattern of advice given by guidance counselors which was, unintentionally, functioning in a discriminatory direction. Negro youngsters who sought guidance were being over-warned by the guidance officers about the unlikelihood of their obtaining professional jobs. They were told of the great discrimination in these areas, and their aspirations were discouraged and directed into more "realistic" spheres, such as becoming postal clerks, policemen, or mechanics. When the Urban League began to win breakthroughs in the professions, so that engineering firms were willing to hire some Negroes, they found a paucity of qualified Negro engineers to be hired.

The psychologists and guidance counselors were not prejudiced. They honestly deplored the job discrimination that prevailed, but, by so accurately appraising the Negro aspirants of the existing situation, they were inadvertently fostering the status quo. In a sense they were saying, "What's the use of getting all excited about training yourself to be a chemist, when you won't be able to get a job when you have the degree?" This seems sensible until one realizes that this argument presumes that discrimination is not going to lessen in the next five years. Nor is the youngster simply informed that the discrimination exists (as though he needs to be told this!), but that perhaps he and other Negroes and whites will be able to do something about breaking down the barriers, so maybe he should go ahead and become the best chemist there is. As a matter of fact, this in itself might be a big blow at discrimination. Instead, the Negro student is warned of all the difficulties ahead of him and this serves to dissuade him. No one can wholeheartedly and spiritedly enter upon a new and difficult path if he considers in detail all the possible obstacles. The guidance officers would have done better to stress the positive, exciting features connected to lively, interesting, professional careers, and in this context motivate the Negro aspirant to overcome the realistically reported difficulties ahead.

Our story is partially dated, however, because in the last few years the Urban League has won its point in many quarters, and a fair proportion of guidance people no longer make this error. Today, the most advanced guidance workers are encouraging professional careers for Negro students. At the same time, the old pattern, in which children are subtly guided away from professional careers because of the prejudice that is envisioned for them by the counselor, has by no means disappeared.

Profile of Patronization: The Soft Approach

Another subtle form of discrimination is patronization in all its guises. While ethnocentrism is no longer common, new forms of condescension have arisen, with a new rationale. Outright rejection of the underpriviliged is frowned upon; rather, it is often suggested that we "accept" them and their culture; that we "understand" their deficiencies as natural, in light of the difficult environment in which they have grown up. There is in this view a great readiness to assume that the underprivileged capitulate to their environment, until we, the teacher, the psychologist, or the social worker, come along to help them. Of course, there is nothing wrong with wanting to help people, so long as it is recognized that they can and have helped themselves. Patronization enters the picture when we fail to see the endemic efforts of the deprived, no matter how devious, to struggle with their environmental difficulties. Only by overlooking their struggles is it possible to feel sorry for them. If we emphasize their weaknesses it is hard not to be condescending.

The specific forms of patronization are manifold: the tendency to talk down to the deprived child—to speak his language, to imitate his slang and speech inflection; the assumption that these children are lacking in intellectual curiosity and conceptual ability; the lowering of academic standards, and the failure to set high goals for the deprived; the too-quick taking for granted that they are not interested in learning.

Much of this is well meant. Academic standards are lowered because it is felt that the educational traditions and aspirations of these children make it impossible for the teacher to demand more.

Thus, many people who defend these practices feel that they are being considerate and sensitive to the needs of these children. Actually, they are being too "understanding" in surrendering to the level at which the child seems to be. Perhaps it is not the disadvantaged who have capitulated to their environment, but the teachers who have capitulated to theirs.

Present-day patronization is essentially rooted in the environmental determinist—or should we say fatalist—rationale. This view, by selectively stressing the negative features of the underprivileged person's environment, arrives at the pessimistic conclusion that these children have basic deficiencies which make it difficult to educate them; therefore, standards must be lowered.

What Can Be Done?

Clearly the problems of discrimination are not going to be solved by decrying the fact that our teachers are of the middle class. Teachers are not going to change their middle-class status, nor is there any reason why they should. And even if more teachers are recruited from lower socio-economic groups—a trend which seems to be taking place in cities like Detroit—they are likely to acquire a middle-class outlook along with their new occupational status.

Good intentions are not sufficient to overcome discrimination, especially unconscious discrimination. As we have seen, discriminatory practices can occur despite the best of intentions.

What, then, can be done? Combating the discrimination requires knowledge as well as good will. First of all, knowledge of the culture of the disadvantaged groups, including specific ethnic differences, is necessary. Beyond this, knowledge of the various forms of discrimination, covert and overt, as well as of ways of counteracting them, is required.

Only by understanding the culture of the underprivileged—and this must include a proper evaluation of strengths and weaknesses—can discrimination be rooted out. Every effort in this direction will bring the middle-class teacher and the deprived child closer together, and, in so doing, remove one of the reasons why Johnny can't learn. There is no need for the teacher to renounce her middle-class role and pretend to imitate the speech or style of the deprived child. He does not want the teacher to become deprived. He is not that pleased with his own situation in life. But he does want the teacher to genuinely understand him, to see that in some way he is grappling with the problems in his life, and not to patronize him. The disadvantaged child wants respect, not love; nor does he want a handout. The only way the teacher can honestly give him respect is by comprehending his way of life and his efforts to overcome the negative aspects of the surrounding environment. Without such understanding, the demand for respect simply has no meaning and becomes another sugar-coated phrase.

iv

THE CULTURE OF THE
UNDERPRIVILEGED:
A NEW LOOK[1]

. . . we will doubtless come to appreciate that some of their [under-privileged groups] values—although strikingly different from those of the dominant groups in our society—are not only utilitarian but worthy of emulation. Many of their patterns of behavior while unacceptable to the majority, may be compatible with successful urban living; others will require modification . . . opinion influencers often confuse adjustment with conformity, believing that only middle-class oriented families can make an effective adaptation to urban life.[2]

Much is unknown about the underprivileged, and still more is controversial. While there are a number of images of lower socio-economic groups, one that is particularly popular today portrays the deprived individual as uncontrolled, aggressive, sexually loose, primitive, and insensitive. This image is frequently found in the writings of Tennessee Williams, and has been portrayed on the screen by Marlon Brando. It is the Blackboard Jungle picture. It is a dangerous image from the point of view of achieving constructive educational changes. A teacher going into a school in an underprivileged neighborhood with this picture in mind is likely to be pessimistic, cynical, and afraid.

While some deprived individuals are undoubtedly impulsive, disorganized, apathetic, violent, depraved, unintelligent—charac-

[1] Portions of the present chapter were presented in a joint paper with S.M. Miller before the American Sociological Association, New York, 1960, and also appear in *Social Problems*, Summer, 1961, pp. 86–97.
[2] Robert C. Weaver, "Human Values of Urban Life," *Proceedings of the Academy of Political Science*, May, 1960, p. 35, 39.

teristics that frequently have been attributed to this group—these traits are not necessarily characteristic of the culture.

Moreover, focusing on the negative side to the exclusion of other, potentially healthy, traits, prevents teachers from developing good relationsships with culturally deprived children and their parents. Consequently, we will attempt to emphasize some of the less observed, more positive themes of this culture, while treating the negative factors in a secondary fashion.

It is, of course, impossible to sketch an entire culture in one chapter; it is possible, however, to outline those features that are relevant to the social practitioner and educator. At the conclusion of this chapter, some of the action implications for the educator are specifically indicated.

In attempting to understand a culture, it is important to see how the customs are transmitted through the family to the child. Thus, a part of our emphasis will be on the family and the child rearing practices; this will be presented in the following chapter. But many aspects of a culture are, at best, only indirectly expressed in the family life. Consequently, before discussing family practices, we will present an over-all view of some of the outstanding characteristics of the culture of the deprived, some of which are in contradiction to each other. The contradictory traits result partly from the fact that the deprived individual is affected not only by his own group but also by the larger society of which he is also a member.

A Portrait of the Underprivileged

He is traditional, "old fashioned" in many ways, patriarchal,[3] superstitious, somewhat religious, though not so religious as his wife.

He reads ineffectively, is poorly informed in many areas, and is often suggestible, although, interestingly enough, he is frequently suspicious of "talk" and "newfangled ideas."

While there are numerous areas about which he is confused and lacking in opinion (e.g., a high percentage of "no answer" and "don't know" on public opinion polls), there are important spheres in which the deprived person has definite, intense con-

[3] The deprived culture is essentially male-centered, with the exception of a major section of the Negro sub-culture which is matriarchal.

victions and, indeed, is difficult to move. His beliefs about morality, punishment, custom, diet, traditional education (in contrast to progressive education, which he firmly rejects), the role of women, intellectuals, are illustrative here. Many of these attitudes are related to his traditional orientation and they are held unquestioningly in the typical traditional manner. They are not open to reason and they are not flexible opinions.

Frequently, the deprived individual feels alienated, not fully a part of society, left out, frustrated in what he can do. This alienation is expressed in a ready willingness to believe in the corruptness of leaders, and a generally antagonistic feeling toward "big shots."

The average underpriviliged person is not individualistic, introspective, self-oriented, or concerned with self-expression. It is unlikely that he will embrace an outlook that prefers moderation, balance, seeing all sides of an issue.

He holds the world, rather himself, responsible for his misfortunes; consequently, he is much less apt to suffer pangs of self-blame, and can be more direct in his expressions of aggression.

Since he sees problems as being caused externally rather than internally, he is more likely to be a poor patient in psychotherapy.

While desiring a better standard of living, he is not attracted to a middle-class style of life, with its accompanying concern for status, prestige, and individualistic methods of betterment. A need for "getting by" rather than "getting ahead" in the self-realization and advancement sense is likely to be dominant. He prefers jobs that promise security to those that entail risk. He does not want to become a foreman because of the economic insecurity resulting from the loss of job seniority.

He is not class conscious, and while he is somewhat radical on a few economic issues, he is distinctly illiberal on numerous matters, particularly civil liberties and foreign policy. He is not interested in politics, does not vote a good deal of the time, and generally belongs to few organizations.

With regard to democracy, he seems to have two sets of attitudes which, on occasion, conflict. He tends to favor the underdog and his relationships to people are marked by an equalitarian, outspoken informality.[4] He is strongly anti-communist, but he does possess a number of traits that have authoritarian potential: he likes strong leaders; he is prejudiced and intolerant; he is less likely to see the need for having dissident opinions.

He sets great store by his family and his personal comforts.

He has an informal, human quality of easy, comfortable relationship to people where the affectionate bite of humor is appreciated. The factory "horseplay," the ritualistic kidding, is part of this pattern. He emphasizes personal qualities. It is the man, not the job, that is important.

The neighbor who gets ahead is expected "not to put on airs"; he should continue to like the "old gang" and accept them despite his new position. An individual is expected to transcend his office. A foreman is an S.O.B., not because he is subject to stresses and demands on the job that force him to act harshly, but because of his personal qualities. Contrariwise, one of the top executives is frequently regarded as one who would help the rank-and-file if he had the chance because he is "a nice guy."

At the political level, the candidate as a decent, human person is more important than the platform.

The deprived individual likes excitement, likes to get away from the humdrum of daily life. News, gossip, new gadgets, sports, are consequently attractive. To some extent, his desire to have new goods, whether television sets or cars, is part of this excitement dimension. The excitement theme is often in contradiction to the traditional orientation.[5]

He is pragmatic and anti-intellectual. It is the end result that counts. What can be seen and felt is more likely to be real and true in his perspective. His practical orientation does not encourage abstract ideas. Education, for what it does for one in terms of opportunities, may be desirable, but abstract, intellectual speculation, ideas that are not rooted in the realities of the present, are not useful, and indeed may be harmful. On the other hand,

---

[4] He is not equalitarian in his relationship to women as his culture is predominatly patriarchal. In the portion of the Negro sub-culture which is matriarchal, the male–female relationships seem more equalitarian.

[5] It is perhaps worth noting that different sub-groups may favor one theme rather than another. Thus, younger groups, and especially juvenile delinquents, are probably much more attracted to the excitement theme, are more alienated, and less traditional.

he may have an exaggerated respect for the ability of the learned. A person with intellectual competence in one field is frequently thought of as a "brain," with ability in all fields.

The anti-intellectualism of the underprivileged individual is one of his most significant handicaps. It is expressed in his feeling that life is a much better teacher than books—theory is impractical, "most big ideas that look good on paper won't work in practice," "talk is bull," intellectuals are "phony eggheads." This anti-intellectualism seems to be rooted in a number of the traits that characterize him: his physical style, alienation, antagonism to the school, defensiveness regarding his gullibility, and his generally pragmatic outlook.

The deprived individual appears to learn in what Miller and Swanson describe as a much more physical or motoric fashion. "Some people can think through a problem only if they can work on it with their hands. Unless they can manipulate objects physically, they cannot perform adequately. Other people (symbolic learners) feel more comfortable if they can get a picture of the task and then solve it in their heads. They may be handicapped in attacking problems that require a motoric orientation."[6]

This difference in approach or style of life is expressed in many areas. In religion, for example, the deprived individual is much more likely to enjoy physical manifestations of emotions such as hand clapping and singing, in contrast to the more dignified sermon. Miller and Swanson note also that when the deprived individual becomes mentally ill, he is more likely to develop symptoms such as conversion hysteria and catatonia, which involve malfunctions of the voluntary muscles. Middle-class individuals, by contrast, more often develop symptoms such as obsessions and depressions, which are characterized by inhibition of voluntary movements and by ruminative attempts to figure out solutions to conflict.[7]

Another reflection of the physical orientation is to be found in the deprived individual's admiration for strength and endurance, two of his principal economic assets. His great interest in sports, and admiration for prize fighters and baseball heroes, is one

[6] Daniel R. Miller and Guy E. Swanson, *Inner Conflict and Defense* (New York: Henry Holt, 1960), p. 24.
[7] *Ibid.*, pp. 310–311.

reflection of his attitude toward physical prowess. This interest may stem, in part, from a way of life that calls for considerable "ruggedness." The man who stands up well under these difficult conditions of life is well thought of. Furthermore, the status-giving attribute of strength is not easily usurped by other groups. This represents one possible line of achievement respected to some extent by other classes, although perhaps for different reasons.

Closely related to this physical bias is the emphasis on masculinity. The underprivileged boy's emphasis on masculinity derives, in part, from his patriarchal culture where the father is the "tough boss" of the home, and his authority is backed up by physical force. Even in the Negro sub-culture, the mother frequently plays a strong, masculine type of role, and is prone to stress and utilize physical force.

Talk, reading, and intellectualism in general are viewed as unmasculine—the opposite of action. Moreover, the school is often imaged as a "prissy" place dominated by women and female values.[8]

Some Action Implications

The implications for the educator to be presented here are not intended to be all-inclusive, but rather are illustrative of what might be done with an awareness of the culture of the underprivileged.

The New Reader. There is a great need for readers and materials more attuned to the experiences and problems of lower socio-economic groups. The textbooks used in the school present predominantly middle-class illustrations, rarely concerning themselves with problems or heroes of the disadvantaged. Ralph Tyler states this issue well:

> The fact that writers of textbooks and teachers have come from a fairly restricted middle-class environment may account to a great extent for the limiting of the content of elementary school reading materials and of the books used in other subjects to those aspects of life which are largely middle-class in char-

[8] Sexton discusses this issue in detail and refers to the "female school." See Patricia Sexton, *Education and Income* (New York: The Viking Press, Inc., 1961), p. 278.

acter. Elementary school books do not deal with homes as they are known by a large percentage of American children. The books in use treat of business, industry, politics, and the professions, usually in terms of the white-collar participant, rather than in terms that would be most understandable to a large fraction of the children.[9]

Also the readers used in the fifth grade for children who are "retarded" in reading, ordinarily are not appropriate for children of this age. New books must be developed that will interest these slow readers, to replace materials prepared for children who read at the first grade level. It should not be assumed that these readers would contain the negative features of the deprived person's life such as slums and the like; instead, they could reflect the most positive aspects of the culture, e.g., the cooperative family traditions, the humor, the informality.

Some readers, or, more accurately, some stories in current use are relatively more popular than others with deprived children. These should be discovered and encouraged.

School Know-How. Disadvantaged children are especially deficient in what might be called "school know-how." By this is meant the subtle expectations concerning various procedures in the school about which the average middle-class child usually learns, without realizing it, from his parents and general environment. By contrast, the deprived child frequently has not learned how to ask and answer questions, how to study, how to relate to the teacher, how to take tests. Frequently, he does not understand the meaning of phrases like "is to" (cat "is to" kitten as lion "is to" cub). These difficulties hamper the child tremendously in the school system. Teachers should not take this school know-how for granted, but rather should teach it explicitly. This point has value for guidance counselors also. The deprived student who would like to go to college has little knowledge of how to apply for admission, how to fill out forms, how to behave in an interview.

The teacher should carefully explain the uses to which education can be put. She should not assume, as she well might with

[9] Ralph W. Tyler, "Can Intelligence Tests Be Used to Predict Educability?", in *Intelligence and Cultural Differences*, by Kenneth Eells, et al., (Chicago: University of Chicago Press, 1951), p. 45.

a non-deprived child, that the value of education is abundantly clear. Her exposition should take place in the context of the different needs of the deprived, rather than emphasizing the role of education for self-expression and the like. The worth-whileness of education in terms of obtaining various kinds of jobs, dealing with red tape, warding off manipulation and understanding the world, should be accented. The deprived child has little information about what college is like, or the kinds of jobs he can get with higher education.

Action Speaks Louder. The deprived individual is most interested in learning the fundamentals: the three R's and the physical sciences. Far less interest is shown in art, music, and the social studies, as currently taught. New approaches to teaching these subjects must be found. Perhaps music forms more attractive to the disadvantaged, such as spirituals, jazz, and blues, could be introduced more frequently in music courses. Ethnic considerations in relation to art, music, and the social studies could also be taken advantage of more fully. For example, Negro history probably would interest Negro children, and might serve as a good *opener* for the development of further interest in history and the social studies in general.

It is easy enough to give the underprivileged child various vocational subjects, such as shop, which are attuned to his physical approach; our quest, however, is to find ways of utilizing his physical approach to achieve higher learning. In other words, the objective is not simply to *follow* the level of the child, but to utilize his physical interest as one avenue for *leading* him toward abstract thinking.

There are numerous techniques appropriate for the physically-oriented slow learner: role-playing can be utilized in countless ways such as acting out a history lesson (George Washington signing the Constitution), teaching arithmetic and economics by playing "store" and "bank." The role-playing itself is a marvelous stimulus for discussion, and it appeals to the deprived child's love of action. It provides for a much more vivid presentation and fits in with his desire for excitement and movement. The teacher, however, has to develop discussion out of the role-playing scene, and not simply capitulate to children's enjoyment of the acting-out process. The role-playing should be a trigger for advanced discussion and thinking, not a substitute for it.

The new teaching machines developed by B. F. Skinner at Harvard should also be especially effective with deprived children, in light of their physical learning tendencies and their admiration for machines. Standard mechanical devices, such as the tachistoscope, might prove congenial, and even result in improved reading.

There are, of course, a great many physical and visual techniques already in operation in the school—the abacus, the magnetic board, the laboratory demonstration, to mention but a few. Our point is that these techniques are uniquely appropriate for culturally deprived children and should be used as springboards for stimulating thinking at every possible point.

To elucidate the problem even further, let us cite a few examples: in teaching a deprived child about a cat, it would be useful to have him draw a cat, "act out" a cat, write the word on the board, and handle pictures of cats. Similarly, in discussing a musical record the child should be encouraged to put the record on the phonograph and to take it off. Trivial as this example may appear, it is still useful because it points up the need to involve the child's motor muscles in every conceivable fashion. For the same reason, calisthenics introduced at various times in the classroom have a surprisingly beneficial effect.

Anti-Intellectualism. The anti-intellectualism of the deprived individual has to be combated vigorously. Thus, in appealing to the interest of the child it is important not to remain at his level but to work toward higher levels of intellectual appreciation. It is good to arouse his interest in history by discussing a cowboy movie, but the teacher then has to go on to *educate* the child, not simply to entertain him by indulging his interests.

However, this approach is far from sufficient in dealing with the deeply rooted anti-intellectualism that needs to be fought on all fronts. The most fundamental approach with the deprived person is to show him that ideas and theories have practical merit. This can be done more easily in the sciences where he has already manifested interest. It need not occur only in the sciences, however. One teacher told us of an instance where deprived children came to appreciate the value of theory in music. She began by playing many popular records. Then she found a classical piece in which there was a musical phrase similar to one found in a popular song. By contrasting the two pieces she was able to initiate a discussion of the musical form of theme and variation. Some of the more interested students who had attempted to write a few tunes were much impressed with how much more could be accomplished through the study of music theory.

Another line of approach is to highlight intellectual heroes. Examples here might include: Pasteur, Darwin, Frederick Douglas, Booker T. Washington, Freud, Einstein, Salk, Schweitzer, Madame Curie. The lives of these people, as well as the nature of their work, should be discussed in a personal, lively manner.

Masculinize the School. Sexton notes that the culture of the school is essentially female, and that this runs counter to the predominantly masculine values of the underprivileged boy:

> It has been observed that school culture is typically 'polite, prissy, and puritanical' and that there is little place in this female culture for some of the high-ranking values of boy-culture—courage, loyalty, independence—or the high-ranking interests of boys, as sports (except in gym class), outdoor life, popular music, adventure, sex, action.[10]

The masculine values of the underprivileged youngsters lead them to reject the eager beaver, the apple polisher who is so dependent on teacher approval. Conformity, dependence, neatness, non-aggression—major values in the female school—are not consistent with the masculine stress on vigor and independence. Even the novels assigned reflect "the teachers' nice Victorian world of *Silas Marner*, *David Copperfield*, *Ivanhoe*, *Jane Eyre*, *Little Women*, etc."[11]

Sexton suggests that since boys are not too interested in fiction or the "make-believe world of the average school storybook, they should be encouraged, as they seldom are, to read what they have a natural interest in—sports pages and books, adventure stories, science fiction, simple biographies of vigorous males and

[10] Sexton, *op. cit.*, p. 278.
[11] *Op. cit.*, p. 259.

(in higher grades), books that deal frankly with the facts of life."[12]

In light of the "female school" it is no wonder that boys get into trouble in school more frequently than do girls, and that delinquent gangs stress masculinity and anti-school attitudes as core values.

The increasing trend toward more male teachers is an important step in the direction of counter-balancing the "female school." Every effort should be made to encourage the kind of man with whom these youngsters can identify to enter the teaching profession, and to accept positions in schools in underprivileged areas.[13] But hiring men is not enough. The entire school needs increased masculinization—from the reading assigned to the manners required.

[12] *Op. cit.*, p. 259.
[13] Sexton, *op. cit.*, p. 275.

THE SIGNIFICANCE

OF THE FAMILY

The negative side of the underprivileged family is easy to see: the family may be prematurely broken by divorce, desertion, and death; the home is overcrowded, the housing facilities inadequate; considerable economic insecurity prevails; both parents frequently work, and thus the children may be neglected; and typically the irritable, tired parents use physical punishment in order to maintain discipline.

But there is another side of the family which should not be ignored. Two things stand out immediately: there are many children, and there are many parents or parent substitutes. The home typically includes aunts, uncles, and grandparents, all of whom may, to some degree, play a parental role. This pattern is technically known as "the extended family." In the Negro family the grandmother often plays a most decisive role. This is well portrayed in the play, "A Raisin in the Sun."

The key to much of the family life is security and protection. The large extended family provides a small world in which one is accepted and safe. If help is needed, the family is the court of first resort and will provide it, at least to some extent. Time and energy, rather than money, are the chief resources provided. Hand-me-down clothes may be passed on to needy members; the mother's sister may work a little extra to supplement the limited budget. But it is in the providing of the services of helping with children or in the household generally that major aid is provided.

One of the reasons why some underprivileged parents like to have many children seems to be related to the role the family plays as a security-giving agency. The family is seen as a major source of strength in a difficult, unstable world.

Many commentators have placed considerable importance on broken homes as the source of emotional instability, mental illness, juvenile delinquency, and the like. The broken home, however, may not, among the deprived, imply family disorganization (nor does it necessarily have the same implications for a deprived child that it might in a middle-class home). To think of the underprivileged family as consisting of a father, mother, and children alone is to miss vital aspects of this family today.

The Family-Centered Home

The home is a crowded, busy, active, noisy place where no one child is focused upon. There are too many children for this, and the parents have too little time. Consequently, the children spend much more time in each other's company and with the relatives. Individualism and self-concern on the part of the children is much less likely to emerge and is, in fact, discouraged in this more family-centered home.

Intense parent–child relationships are infrequent, and while the danger of parental rejection is present, overprotection is out of the question.

The atmosphere is much more communal and, to some extent, cooperative. For example, it is not at all uncommon to see a six- or seven-year-old child taking his younger brother across the street, holding him by the hand and watching for cars. Nor is it rare to see a mother buy an ice cream cone which she passes from one child to the other to share.

Sibling rivalry and fear of a new baby brother seem to develop somewhat less here. Perhaps this is because the children never have had that much attention in the first place, and have less to lose. Perhaps, also, the fact that the children depend so much on contact with each other, rather than being overly dependent upon the parents, plays a decisive role. Whatever the reason, there does appear to be far less jealousy and competitiveness.

In light of the different structure of the family and the lack of intense parent–child relationships, many of the classic psychoanalytic formulations, such as the Oedipus complex, may have to be revised when viewing the underprivileged.

Discipline and Love

While the last ten years have produced conflicting evidence and opposing interpretations[1] of various aspects of the child rearing of the deprived, there is one area, at least, in which all the evidence agrees. This concerns the parental use of physical punishment as a major source of discipline. This, of course, reflects the traditional approach to life, as well as the physical style of the deprived.

The possibly deleterious effects of punishment have been well argued: it may result in a negative attitude toward the person who administers the punishment; it generally does not develop a flexible, reasoned understanding of why the proscribed behavior is wrong; frequently it is ineffective in halting the forbidden practice; it can be debasing to the dignity of the recipient; it can eventuate in deep, frustrated feelings and latent aggression. Undoubtedly many of these potential consequences affect the deprived child in the expected fashion.

But in recent years the attitude of psychologists toward punishment has changed somewhat. Dr. Benjamin Spock writes:

> In the olden days children were spanked plenty, and nobody thought much about it. Then a reaction set in, and many parents decided that it was shameful. But that didn't settle everything.

[1] The data on weaning and toilet training are omitted in this chapter, largely because of the contradictory nature of the findings. In 1945 Davis and Havighurst reported that the deprived had more "permissive" weaning and toilet training practices than the middle class. In 1954 Maccoby and Gibbs reported that there is no significant class difference for these variables although their general findings show the deprived to be less permissive. In 1960 Miller and Swanson reported data indicating, in support of the earlier Davis and Havighurst findings, that the deprived start toilet training and weaning at a later age. See Allison Davis, and Robert J. Havighurst, "Social Class and Color Differences in Child Rearing," *American Sociological Review*, April, 1953, pp. 142–149. Eleanor E. Maccoby *et al.*, "Methods of Child Rearing in Two Social Classes," in William E. Martin and Celia B. Stendler, *Readings in Child Development* (New York: Harcourt, Brace & Company, 1954). Daniel R. Miller and Guy E. Swanson, *Inner Conflict and Defense* (New York: Henry Holt, 1960).

If an angry parent keeps himself from spanking, he may show his irritation in other ways, for instance, by nagging the child for half the day, or trying to make him feel deeply guilty. I'm not particularly advocating spanking, but I think it is less poisonous than lengthy disapproval, because it clears the air for both parent and child.[2]

Psychological research now indicates that under certain conditions punishment can be effective and anticipated negative consequences may not necessarily occur. This is true if the punishment is not too severe or overpowering, and if alternative actions are available to substitute for the punished acts.[3]

In their recent study, Miller and Swanson found that it is mixed discipline (a combination of physical and psychological forms of discipline) that has the best consequences. They state that boys trained in this manner are more "realistic," "are neither uncontrolled or overly constricted." Their data indicate that while the underprivileged use more physical punishment, and the middle class more psychological techniques (e.g., withholding of love), the mixed form of discipline occurs more frequently among the deprived.[4]

Since physical punishment is part of the everyday pattern among the disadvantaged, there is probably considerable adaptation to it and it is not perceived as a major threat to the ego; as physical punishment and aggression generally are expressed rather easily and directly, it is unlikely that they have the sadistic overtones that often produce the negative correlates of punishment.

Although the consequences of punishment may not necessarily be bad, the question of its effectiveness as a deterrent to proscribed behavior is a different issue. Punishment is apparently ineffective in deterring aggression. Not only does it fail to halt aggressive behavior in deprived children, but in some cases it actually leads to an increase in this behavior. On the other hand, punishment seems to be successful in stopping masturbation, thumb sucking, dependency, and numerous other behaviors dis-

[2] Benjamin Spock, *The Common Sense Book of Baby and Child Care*, (New York: Duell, Sloan & Pearce, Inc., 1957).

[3] Clifford Morgan, *Introduction to Psychology*, (New York: McGraw Hill Book Co., Inc., 1956), p. 115.

[4] Daniel R. Miller and Guy E. Swanson, *Inner Conflict and Defense*, (New York: Henry Holt, 1960), pp. 399, 426.

approved by lower socio-economic groups.

Since punishment appears to be so effective in these areas, why is it notoriously ineffective in preventing aggression among the underprivileged? A number of possibilities suggest themselves in light of the culture of the deprived. First, there seems to be considerable ambivalence toward aggression in this culture. While it is rejected as a form of response to the parents and family, it is expected that the child will stand up for himself, and fight if necessary, in the outer environment. Secondly, the parents themselves express anger in administering physical punishment. In a sense, they provide a model for imitation. Although they tell the child not to be aggressive, they themselves are aggressive in punishing him. They appear to be saying, "Do as I say but not as I do."

Why do underprivileged parents use punishment so freely? This practice is frequently interpreted as restrictive and unloving. However, with the peculiar problems that plague their lives, with large families often crowded into small apartments, and with both parents working, the problem of discipline becomes a difficult one. Popularly held notions of permissiveness cannot easily be applied. Respect and obedience without a lot of arguing and "reasoning" is probably much more convenient when the parents come home tired from a hard day's work. They are in no mood to cajole the children and they resort much more quickly to physical punishment—not sadistic beatings, but a quick slap and a strong tone.

A number of studies have noted that deprived individuals strongly, and more frequently, support the statement that "the most important thing a child should learn is respect and obedience to his parents."[5] Not only parents, but older people in general are to be obeyed and respected. After all, if neighbors and relatives, including grandparents, are to take part in child rearing, respect for older people is important.

Underprivileged people do not see discipline as inconsistent with love; that is, they do not feel when they punish a child that this might indicate a lack of love for him.

"Love," the keynote of middle-class child rearing, plays a much

[5] Frank Riessman, *Workers' Attitudes Toward Participation and Leadership*, unpublished Ph.D. dissertation, Columbia University, 1955.

less central role among the deprived, where it is taken for granted and not something that the child must win, nor something that he loses by disobeying. If the child is "bad" he gets a "belt" rather than a conversation. He is not told that "Mommy won't love him if he isn't good."

Control of children is not exerted by the withholding of love but through punishment. A child is expected to do what he is told, not because he wants to demonstrate love for his parents; rather, he does it because it is expected, and if he does not do it he will be punished. He does not accrue love by doing, nor lose it by not doing.

The meaning of love is different where it must be earned and where it is regarded as involved in all one does. A reprimand can then seem to indicate a lack of love by the parent. It need not have this meaning where parental authority is unquestioned and children are expected to perform their roles without the reward or deprivation of love.

When a child disobeys and his mother "whacks" him, he knows what he is being punished for, and it is soon over. His mother has indicated that she disapproves of his behavior but, because she has not threatened him with the loss of love, it would seem the child is assured of her continued feeling for him.

Functional Responsibility

Davis and Havighurst found that middle-class parents expect their children to learn to cook, sew, help in the house, and generally assume responsibility at an earlier age than do underprivileged parents.[6] Other studies also indicate that the deprived child is not expected to pick up his own toys, or put away his own clothes, at as early an age as his middle-class counterpart. Middle-class respondents when interviewed stated that the child should be on his own as early as possible.

These findings are surprising in light of the fact that deprived children are expected to get jobs after school at an earlier age, and often they appear older and more mature. Moreover, since

[6] Allison Davis and Robert J. Havighurst, "Social Class and Color Differences in Child Rearing," in *Readings in Social Psychology* by Guy E. Swanson, Theodore M. Newcomb, and Eugene L. Hartley, 2nd edition, (New York: Henry Holt, 1952), p. 539–550.

both parents work and are likely not to be at home as much, one would expect that the children would be given more household assignments as part of the division of labor that characterizes the extended family.

How then can the findings of Davis and Havighurst be explained? The authors themselves have an illuminating interpretation.

> The explanation probably lies in a tendency on the part of middle-class people to train their children early for achievement and responsibility, while lower-class people train their children to take responsibility only after the child is old enough to make the effort of training pay substantial returns in the work the child will do. Middle-class parents can afford to use time to train children . . . at such an early age that the children cannot repay this training effort by their actual performance, although they may repay it by adopting attitudes of self-achievement and responsibility.[7]

The deprived apparently are more concerned with what might be termed functional responsibility rather than symbolic training for the future.

Another indication of functional responsibility training is found in a study reported by Bronfenbrenner.[8] Here middle-class children were taught to *start* dressing and feeding themselves at an earlier age than deprived children. However, the deprived child was able to *completely* feed and dress himself earlier than the middle-class child. The mother of the underprivileged child apparently introduced the training at an age where it could be effective, while the middle-class parent was satisfied to have the child make some effort at dressing and feeding, in a sense, looking

---

[7] *Ibid.*, p. 549.

[8] Bronfenbrenner does not share Davis and Havighurst's view of the data on responsibility. He simply summarizes all the data showing that the middle-class parents, in general, expect their children to pick up their toys at an earlier age, cook earlier, etc. As the majority of the items are in this direction, he is able to conclude that the lower class demands less responsibility. It is only by observing contradictions among the items that Davis and Havighurst were able to develop their interpretation. See Urie Bronfenbrenner, "Socialization and Social Class Through Time and Space," in *Readings in Social Psychology* by Eleanor E. Maccoby, Theodore M. Newcomb, and Eugene L. Hartley, third edition, (New York: Henry Holt, 1958), pp. 400–425.

responsible and independent even though this served no immediate functional purpose.

The Question of Sex

The attitude of the deprived toward sex is something of an enigma. Much of the evidence is, on the surface, contradictory. On the one hand there is Kinsey's well-known data which indicate that premarital intercourse is far more frequent among lower socio-economic groups.[9] Teachers' observations that pregnancy is more common among teen-age girls in culturally deprived areas is in the same direction. Common-law marriages and broken homes are certainly more frequent also. On the other hand, there is evidence that does not fit into this picture as neatly. Doctors working in poor neighborhoods have told us that these women have a more puritanical, inhibited attitude toward sex. This seems to be confirmed by a recent study in Chicago by Lee Rainwater.[10] Moreover, Kinsey's data show that the women, unlike the men, do not have more frequent premarital sex relations.

Various studies indicate that deprived parents are much less likely to permit their children to walk around naked in the house, and they are less apt to appear unclothed in front of their children.[11] The studies also reveal that these families, far from encouraging indulgence of the child's sexual play with himself, are more concerned than middle-class parents with preventing masturbation. (This effort *may* be undesirable, but it certainly does not indicate any easy indulgence of the impulses of the child.) The deprived child is much more likely to be punished for masturbatory acts than is the middle-class child (whose parents may be more attuned to the new demands of permissive upbringing).

Some recent research has brought into question another attitude toward sexual practices. It has been widely accepted that illegitimacy is more widespread among lower socio-economic

[9] Alfred C. Kinsey, *et al.*, *Sexual Behavior in the Human Male*, (Philadelphia: Saunders, 1948).

[10] Lee Rainwater, *And the Poor Get Children*, (Chicago: Quadrangle Books, Inc., 1961).

[11] Robert R. Sears *et al.*, *Patterns of Child Rearing*, (Evanston: Row, Peterson & Company, 1957), Chapter VI.

groups. The California studies of Clark Vincent on unwed mothers raise some doubt about this belief.[12] Vincent found that illegitimacy among the deprived was far greater than among the middle class, if one examined the public hospital records, but that *illegitimate births among middle-class individuals were far* more frequent when data were collected from private doctors. Data on abortions are, of course, much more difficult to obtain, although Kinsey's data suggest that abortion has become a common practice in all classes.

After examining these contradictory findings and impressions, it is most difficult to arrive at any clear-cut, unambiguous conclusion, but a few tentative interpretations are possible. The attitude toward nudity in the home can perhaps best be explained in terms of the crowded living conditions characteristic of deprived life. If the parents and children sleep in the same room, and a number of children sometimes sleep in the same bed, a permissive attitude toward nudity might prove dangerous. Similarly, the strong parental inhibition of masturbation may be rooted in the close living arrangements of the family.

These attitudes indicate a strong taboo against sexual behavior. If this is true, how can we explain the frequently observed pregnancies among adolescent girls? This is a difficult question. In attempting to answer it, perhaps first we should assume that the conditions of deprived life—limited supervision of children, crowded homes—produce a strain toward sexual behavior at an earlier age. To some extent the parents may recognize this danger and attempt to counteract it. This effort is expressed in their attitudes toward nudity, masturbation, and the like. But sometimes the life conditions are too powerful and overcome the inhibitions. When this takes place, and pregnancy results, the attitude seems to be one of resignation and both the girl and the child are accepted as part of the family.

Recently at a P.T.A. meeting, a Negro woman made a distinction about illegitimacy which many of us may not be aware of. In her eyes the worst thing an unwed mother could do would be to surrender the child to an adoption agency. Abortion also was looked upon with some disfavor. Keeping the illegitimate child

[12] Clark E. Vincent, "The Unwed Mother and Sampling Bias," *American Sociological Review*, October, 1954, pp. 562–567.

and accepting the responsibility was the most favored solution to this difficult problem. It is not to be covered up, "hypocritically denied," once the mistake has been made. Unfortunately this is often misunderstood by the outside observer, who sees illegitimacy as going hand in hand with a light and "irresponsible" attitude toward marriage. The deprived, just as the middle class, prefer legitimate children in legitimate marriages. When something goes wrong, and this apparently occurs in all classes according to the statistics, the deprived prefer to incorporate the child in the household and to accept the attendant responsibilities.

There are a few other dimensions to the attitude toward sex. The traditionalism of the underprivileged is an important factor in contributing to the more puritanical attitudes, and to the patriarchal feature expressed in the greater freedom for the male (evidenced by Kinsey's findings). To some extent, the traditionalism is counterbalanced, particularly among the younger groups, by the search for excitement, and sex is a well-promoted avenue for this search.

Another consideration is the fact that the deprived adolescent is far more of an adult in that he is already employed or anticipates working in a short time, and he is much less dependent on his parents. Under these circumstances it is more likely that he will engage in adult sexual practices at an earlier age.

Finally, there are sub-groups differences among the deprived that have to be taken into account in understanding the sexual mores. For example, a large section of the Negro group has a matriarchal family structure where the mother and grandmother play powerful roles. The attitude toward sex is likely to be somewhat different in this setting than in the more typically patriarchal cultures.

While we feel we have shed some light on the sexual attitudes of the deprived, it must be confessed that there is still much that is unclear.

Action Implications

Teachers, P.T.A. leaders, and school administrators should recognize the significance of the "extended" family and utilize it in the attempt to effect changes in the child. For example, in considering college for the economically deprived child, guidance counselors should recognize that the family will frequently pool its resources and take extra jobs in order to send *one* of the children to college.

Instead of absorbing blame, the family, if worked with properly, can perhaps play a powerful role in combating juvenile delinquency. Thus, strong efforts should be made to enlist the aid of members of the extended family.

Juvenile delinquency is often explained, in an oversimplified manner, as resulting from broken families and insufficient love and attention. If we recognize the role of the larger family we cannot accept this explanation quite so readily.

The teacher should work closely with the family, and through respecting it, build a basis of mutual respect which the parents can help transfer to the child. Suggestions from the family should be encouraged and *acted upon*. Too often suggestions are elicited from parents in the course of attempting to establish good relations with them, only to be forgotten or ignored later. A great deal can be learned from the parents about the community, ethnic differences, and cultural traditions.

In this connection, a new position has been developed in a number of school systems, called School–Community Coordinator, whose job it is to interpret the school to the parents, and interpret the *parents to the school*. To be successful, he has to be a two-way communicator.[13]

Respect vs. Love

While underprivileged children strongly desire physical warmth, it would be a mistake to believe that they want intense affection. Very often teachers from a non-deprived background misread a child's desire for physical expression and assume that it is "love" that he wants.

Deprived children need respect rather than "love" from their teacher. The teacher need not be a substitute parent! Love is not a major issue in the deprived home; it is not used as a discipline technique, and the child generally does not feel that he

[13] In some areas there is a Puerto Rican Community Coordinator, whose special function it is to integrate the school and the Puerto Rican community, interpreting each to the other. In some cases these coordinators are not highly trained people, but rather "informal leaders" who have close ties to the neighborhood and its traditions.

must win love or that he can lose it. Respect, on the other hand, is something that the child is not likely to have received in the culture at large. This lack of respect is closely connected to his feelings of alienation and resentment. Too many people (in society at large) deprecate him and laugh at him. He himself knows that he is ignorant. He needs a teacher who will stand by him, someone on whom he can depend. For him to be accepted despite his initial hostility and defiance is paramount.

The Problem of Punishment

The fact that the parents of deprived children employ physical punishment as a major source of discipline presents a serious problem for the teacher because this practice is rightly condemned in the school system. Probably the best way the teacher can emulate the parental discipline, without employing corporal punishment, is by being definite, authoritative, "strict." (Classroom "rebellion" is more a reflection of the child's feeling of alienation from the school than a basic reaction to authority.)

The parents of deprived children often punish them by restriction of privileges, and this pattern can easily be imitated by the teacher. The great danger to be avoided is the protracted reasoning and arguing about rules and regulations that is so popular in modern homes, but is most ineffective with the deprived child who has had little of this type of experience. On the other hand, there is a technique that has been employed successfully, which does allow for the discussion of rules. This is the "mock court," in which other children try the offender in a make-believe classroom court. Here the laws can be argued and justice can be explained. But this has to be used carefully, with full preparation of the children involved; otherwise it can become a farce, where the teacher attempts to impose *her* justice.

The Limits of Traditional Psychotherapy

There is now considerable evidence that the standard psychological approaches are not attractive to most deprived people, and, in fact, may be somewhat inappropriate for them. Psychoanalytic formulations in particular require considerable modification in order to be applicable to deprived individuals. Most psychoanalytic therapy is based on the assumption of a middle-class, love-oriented childhood pattern and its presumed repetition in the therapeutic situation. In the light of the different emphasis on love in the deprived family, this may be a misleading assumption. The fact that this family includes many adults ("parent substitutes"), a less intense relationship of child to parent and more sibling contact, also has bearing on psychoanalytic concepts and treatment.

Most psychiatric practice takes place either in the well-furnished office of the therapist, or in a hospital setting. Recently it has been observed that home visits by the psychiatrists to the families of the deprived have led to much improved rapport between patients and doctors. Moreover, the psychiatrists report that they see the problem in a different light when it is observed in the family setting.

Balance Sheet: Strengths and Weaknesses

Drawing up a balance sheet listing strengths and weaknesses of the underprivileged is not an easy task. Although some traits have fairly clear positive or negative consequences, others are more ambiguous. On the liability side of the ledger are: narrowness of traditionalism, pragmatism, and anti-intellectualism; limited development of individualism, self-expression, and creativity; frustrations of alienation; political apathy; suggestibility and naïveté; boring occupational tasks; broken, over crowded homes.

On the asset side are: the cooperativeness and mutual aid that mark the extended family; avoidance of the strain accompanying competitiveness and individualism; equalitarianism, informality, and warm humor; freedom from self-blame and parental overprotection; the children's enjoyment of each other's company, and lessened sibling rivalry; the security found in the extended family and in a traditional outlook.

Much more unclear are the effects of the quest for excitement, the alienation, the stubbornness, the desire for strong leadership, the early marriages, the attitudes toward sex, the role of love, the parent substitutes in the home and the development of Oedipal resolutions, and the effects of corporal punishment.

vi

THE HIDDEN I.Q.[1]

Intelligence tests measure how quickly people can solve relatively un-important problems making as few errors as possible, rather than measuring how people grapple with relatively important problems, making as many productive errors as necessary with time no factor.[2]

A few years ago a birthday party for a member of the staff at a well-known psychological clinic played a novel role in the test performance of a Negro child. Prior to the party this boy, whom we shall call James, had been described on the psycho-logical record as "sullen, surly, slow, unresponsive, apathetic, unimaginative, lacking in inner life." This description was based on his behavior in the clinic interviews and on his performance on a number of psychological measures including an intelligence test and a personality test. His was not an unusual record; many culturally deprived children are similarly portrayed.

On the day of the birthday party, James was seated in an adjoining room waiting to go into the clinician's office. It was just after the lunch hour and James had the first afternoon ap-pointment. The conclusion of the lunch break on this particular day was used by the staff to present a surprise birthday cake to one of the clinicians who happened to be a Negro. The beauti-fully decorated cake was brought in and handed to the recipient by James' clinician who was white, as were all the other mem-bers of the staff. The Negro woman was deeply moved by the

---

[1] In this chapter we are particularly indebted to Walter Murray for permitting us to quote from his unpublished paper, "Some Major Assump-tions Underlying the Development of Intelligence Tests," 1960.
[2] Personal communication to the author from Irving Taylor.

cake—and the entire surprise. In a moment of great feeling, she warmly embraced the giver of the cake. James inadvertently perceived all this from his vantage point in the outer office. That afternoon he showed amazing alacrity in taking the tests and responding in the interview. He was no longer sullen and dull. On the contrary, he seemed alive, enthusiastic, and he answered questions readily. His psychologist was astonished at the change and in the course of the next few weeks retested James on the tests on which he had done so poorly. He now showed marked improvement, and she quickly revised not only the test appraisal of him on the clinical record card, but her general personality description of him as well.

The high point of their new, positive relationship came some months later when he confided to her that she had gotten off on the wrong foot with him on the first day in the first three minutes of contact. She was taken aback and said, "What do you mean? I was very friendly, I told you my name and asked you yours." He responded, "Yeh, and I said James Watson and right away you called me Jimmy and you bin callin' me Jimmy ever since. My name is James, 'cept to my very good friends maybe. Even my mother calls me James." Then he went on to tell her how he had changed his opinion of her on the day of the birthday party because of the close relationship he had seen widened between her and the Negro psychologist.

This little story illustrates a number of things:

First, it shows that *the test is a social situation*. The testing situation, whether it be a psychological test or any other kind of test, for that matter, reflects a relationship between people, a relationship that is often remarkably subtle. And when anything hampers this relationship, the result is likely to show in the test score itself. This can occur on an individual test as well as a group test, an I.Q. test as well as a personality test, a subject matter examination as well as a psychological measure.

It also shows how the behavior evidenced in the clinical situation tends to be seen by the psychologist as indicative of the basic personality of the child. This is frequently done with little awareness of how much this behavior is a product of the particular relationship of the psychologist to the child, and of the testing situation as such. Children from different cultural backgrounds respond very differently to clinical situations and to the idea of being tested or evaluated.

The anecdote also points up the fact that a well-meaning, clinically trained, unprejudiced psychologist can have poor rapport with a deprived child, not because of deficient psychological technique, but because of limited knowledge about certain cultural attitudes. In this case, the attitude in question is the feeling held by many Negro people that the informality intended by shortened nicknames signifies a lack of respect when it takes place across cultural lines. This does not suggest that the child himself was aware of this reasoning, but that, rather, he was simply reflecting his parents' wish that he be called by his full name.

The importance of having Negro psychologists on the staff of a clinic is shown in a pertinent way by the anecdote. The Negro child need not himself have a Negro clinician, but her presence in the clinic was indirectly influential.

Finally, the story neatly illustrates the fact that scores on tests are not fixed and can be reversed dramatically when the relationship to the tester is improved. There is apparently a hidden I.Q. and a hidden personality that is often not revealed by the test and the clinical interview. In our story, James' I.Q. score rose considerably in the retesting and his personality began to appear in a totally new light.

The I.Q. Controversy

Currently there is considerable questioning of some of the basic assumptions of the I.Q. test. Consistent with the incident we have just reported, the old notion that the I.Q. is relatively stable or constant is under heavy fire. There is increasing recognition that I.Q. scores of underprivileged children do not reflect their ability, because the test items include words that are not in the experience repertoire of these children.

But there are many other assumptions involved that have not been as fully questioned, and perhaps it would be a good idea to briefly trace the history of the I.Q. controversy.

At first the issue revolved around whether the lower I.Q. of deprived children was a result of heredity or environment. Research indicated that environmental factors were apparently decisive in producing the higher middle-class I.Q. Then Allison Davis questioned the applicability of the I.Q. tests to deprived groups.[3] He wondered if the tests might not be impregnated with middle-class problems and language, and thus not be fair to underprivileged youngsters.

What Davis did was to take various intelligence test problems on which the deprived did poorly, and reword them in terms equally familiar to all children. For example:

Instead of "Cub is to bear as gosling is to 1 ( ) fox, 2 ( ) grouse, 3 ( ) goose, 4 ( ) rabbit, 5 ( ) duck," he substituted, "Puppy goes with dog like kitten goes with 1 ( ) fox, 2 ( ) goose, 3 ( ) cat, 4 ( ) rabbit, 5 ( ) duck."

The required understanding of the relationship of the concepts is not altered by the revised form. If the child does not know the word "gosling," he can never demonstrate his grasp of the relationship required in this question. In other words, until the change was made, this item was functioning as a vocabulary test for the disadvantaged child.[4] The reformulation changed not only the vocabulary involved, but also the structure of the sentence to read "puppy *goes with* dog like kitten *goes with* ――." "Goes with" is substituted for "is to." This made the problem more understandable to the underprivileged children.

Surprisingly enough, however, even though Davis' changes produced a test that was more attuned to them, disadvantaged youngsters did not improve markedly. Something else apparently was deterring them. It remained for Ernest Haggard to clear up the mystery.[5]

[3] Allison Davis, *Social-Class Influences Upon Learning*, (Cambridge: Harvard University Press, 1948).

[4] Robert Havighurst, one of Davis' colleagues, points out that items requiring knowledge of the following words may touch the experience of the middle-class child but not that of the deprived child: fireplace, chandelier, wall-paper, salad fork, dining room. Words which might be more familiar to deprived children, such as pump, coal stove, kerosene lamp, rain barrel, rarely appear on intelligence tests. Kenneth Eells, *et al.*, *Intelligence and Cultural Differences*, (Chicago: University of Chicago Press, 1951), p. 18.

[5] Ernest A. Haggard, "Social Status and Intelligence," *Genetic Psychology Monographs*, Vol. 49, 1954, pp. 141–186; also personal communications from Dr. Haggard.

The Big Three: Practice, Motivation, Rapport

Haggard reasoned that although deprived children may have taken many I.Q. tests, they really did not know how to take these tests properly: they lacked meaningful, directed practice. They also lacked motivation, and their relationship to the examiner was typically distant and beset by fears.

Haggard decided to control each of these factors. He gave both deprived and non-deprived children three one-hour training periods in taking I.Q. tests. These practice periods included careful explanation of what was involved in each of the different types of problems found on the I.Q. tests. The explanations were given in words that were familiar to both groups. Haggard also offered special rewards for doing well, and he trained his examiners to be responsive to the deprived children as well as to the middle-class youngsters, thus greatly enhancing the rapport.[6]

Under these conditions the I.Q.'s of the disadvantaged children improved sharply. *This occurred with only three hours of practice.*[7] And it occurred even on the old I.Q. tests with the middle-class-biased items. Apparently more important than the content of the test items was the attitude of the children toward the test situation and the examiner.

[6] In the area of motivation, it is clear that middle-class children are more motivated to do well on examinations of the I.Q. sort because of the general emphasis on success and competition in middle class life. Even where an examination is not directly related to a reward or a threat, the middle-class child strives to perform well. Part of the difference in I.Q. scores of middle-class and deprived children is due to differences in strength of motivation to perform well on an examination rather than to differences in intelligence.

This point is indirectly verified in a study by Douvan. At first, an examination was given to both deprived and middle-class youngsters without any indication of its importance, or of an offering of a meaningful reward for satisfactory work. The result was typical: the middle-class group showed far greater motivation than the deprived group. Later, the test was rerun, but this time a reward was offered for successful work on the test. The result: the motivation of the deprived group increased much more than that of the middle-class group. Thus, when the test situation promised rewards that were direct, immediate, practical, and meaningful, deprived children responded at a higher level than where such rewards were absent. But less so with middle-class youth, who are more often motivated to perform at close to their maximum level even while rewards are absent. See Elizabeth Douvan, "Social Status and Success Striving," *Journal of Abnormal and Social Psychology*, March, 1956, pp. 219–223.

[7] Haggard, *op. cit.*

Haggard also showed that when test items were read aloud to the deprived children while they followed in their test booklets, these children did much better.[8] Deprived children are notoriously poor readers. Consequently, their typically inadequate intelligence test performance is partly a result of that difficulty rather than of limited intelligence.

It might be asked at this point, why all the fuss—if deprived children cannot read well, what difference does it make if we say they are less intelligent, or that they are deficient in reading? The answer is that it makes a huge difference because of the contrasting implications of deficiencies in intelligence and deficiencies in reading ability. Reading skill, it is generally accepted, can be improved fairly easily, certainly in the child, and to some degree even in the adult, where motivation is present. On the other hand, the old assumption was that intelligence, while it is affected by experience and knowledge, is much less easily changed or improved. Perhaps not much can be done in schools to help deprived children if they suffer from low intelligence; but the outlook is much more positive if the problem is poor reading.[9]

I.Q. Assumptions Discriminate Against the Deprived

Walter Murray, one of Davis' co-workers, is currently continuing the analysis of basic assumptions underlying the I.Q. He

[8] Haggard, *op. cit.*

[9] It might be objected, of course, that in Haggard's investigation the underprivileged youngsters improved more than did the middle-class because the latter had the higher I.Q. scores and thus could not improve upon them. There are two answers to this objection, one of which is somewhat technical: Haggard points out that through the use of a special statistical method (the Johnson–Neyman technique), the effect of the higher I.Q. of the middle-class children was held constant or removed. (Haggard, personal communication)

Secondly, and less technical, the argument overlooks a fundamental assumption underlying most intelligence tests, namely, that the I.Q. is relatively stable, and that it certainly *cannot be raised easily*. Haggard's study shows, on the contrary, that in a period of five days that included only three one-hour practice sessions, the I.Q. of large numbers of deprived youngsters could be significantly increased. What seems to be involved here is that if the individual or group is not functioning with high motivation, or if efficient test-taking techniques have not been developed, or if rapport with the examiner is not good, the resulting *performance* can rather readily be improved.

questions the following assumptions which function either directly or indirectly to penalize the deprived child:[10]

1. The I.Q. is measured by the use of brief exercises that have to be executed fairly quickly; while "many of the problems that individuals are expected to solve in real life require much time and concentration," this type of task is excluded from the I.Q. test.

The brief exercises and the general accent on speed in particular work against the deprived child. His style is slow and cautious. It takes him a long time to become involved in problems, and his potential will not easily be evidenced on short, speed-oriented tasks. He will, in all likelihood, show his ability only after he is absorbed in a problem. Many non-deprived children have a similar work orientation, of course, and rural children find the speed emphasis equally distasteful.

Allison Davis notes that speed is affected by cultural attitudes concerning the importance or unimportance of speed, and by personality factors, such as "competitiveness, conscientiousness, compulsiveness, exhibitionism, and anxiety."[11] *These personality characteristics are less frequently associated with the deprived child's personality pattern.*

2. The I.Q. score is based on the accuracy of the final answer to the I.Q. question, not the method of thinking involved in arriving at this answer. "In most tests the final score, or judgment of the student's intelligence, is based on the number of correct responses. Little or no attention is given to the method by which the student attacked the problem or the kinds of considerations he made use of in attempting to solve it."[12]

The deprived child does not possess, as one psychologist put it recently, "good avoidance conditioning for wrong answers."

---

[10] Murray, *op. cit.*

[11] *Op. cit.*

[12] Haggard reports the following: "In one study, children were asked to give the reasons for their answers to intelligence test items. In the case of one analogy item, 35 of the 60 children tested marked the "correct" response, but not one of these children gave the "correct" reason for marking it. The reasons given were on the basis of rhyming, synonym, etc., but not on the basis of making the analogy—the process which the test constructor assumed was being measured. Ernest A. Haggard, "Techniques for the Development of Unbiased Tests," *Proceedings: 1952 Conference on Testing Problems*, (Princeton: Educational Testing Service, 1953).

He does not have a good sense for what is likely to be a poor answer because he has limited test-taking skills. The teacher and the psychologist are typically oriented toward getting the right answer, and are less interested in the thinking processes involved, particularly when this thinking does not lead to the correct result.[13]

3. Intelligence is assumed to develop and increase with age; items which do not show an improvement with age are excluded from the I.Q. tests.

The assumption that intelligence increases with age has an indirect effect on the measurement of the I.Q. of the deprived child. Characteristically his measured I.Q. has been found to *fall* with age. This is, apparently, because he has not been exposed to the experiences and vocabulary presumed to be normal in the culture, and on which all the I.Q. tests are based. Now if it were possible to have I.Q. exercises that were not dependent on these experiences, and that measured skills that did not improve with the age of the child, the underprivileged child might fare better.

4. It is assumed that intelligence is best demonstrated in a school environment. I.Q. tests have tended to become tests of scholastic aptitude. Intelligence may be relatively unimportant in business, industry, agriculture, etc., but this does not on the surface appear to be a very sound assumption.

With regard to the highly academic character of the I.Q. test, Ralph Tyler notes that

> . . . so far as problem-solving exercises are concerned the typical intelligence tests lean heavily on academic, school-type problems, whereas lower-class children frequently have had more experience than have middle-class children in dealing with the kinds of practical problems encountered on the street and in the playground. That is to say, it seems clear . . . that youngsters

[13] Haggard reports a study in which "the test constructor wrote out the mental processes he thought were being measured by the items in his published test. It was found that for some items over 50 per cent of the 152 nine- and ten-year-old children gave logically defensible reasons for marking answers considered 'incorrect' by the test constructor. Furthermore, whenever more than one logically defensible answer to an item was given, the middle-class children tended to give the 'correct' answer (in the opinion of the test constructor), whereas lower-class children tended to give the 'incorrect' answer (in the opinion of the test constructor)." See Haggard, *ibid.*

who do not show up well on intelligence tests do possess abilities that indicate some skill in solving practical problems and that suggest potentialities for further education if the schools had broad enough goals to utilize talents of these kinds.[14]

Early Environment and the Changeability of the I.Q.

Few people still maintain the old assumption that the I.Q. is necessarily stable or constant throughout life. There is too much evidence showing that it can be changed under varying conditions. But an allied view has been advanced that is related to the "constancy" assumption.

This argument holds that the underprivileged child has been immersed in an early "impoverished" environment in which there is insufficient stimulation, thus producing a *basic retardation,* so that, in effect, his I.Q. remains relatively low throughout life.[15]

One version of this argument maintains that the early environment of the deprived child produces behavior similar to that sometimes found in institutional children, and in children brought up in isolation from society. At its extreme, this view sees the behavior of deprived children as being similar to that found in the stimulus deprivation experiments, where volunteers are put in special respiratory tanks for twenty-four hours. (Following these experiments, the subjects are unable to concentrate, their I.Q. performance and problem-solving ability temporarily deteriorates, and they are in a general fog.) The stimulus deprivation thesis presumes that the underprivileged child has suffered some similar lack of stimulation over a long period of time, particularly in his early life, and that this accounts for his low I.Q. There are three levels at which this argument may be challenged:

1. In the first place, the stimulus-depriving tank analogy seems

[14] Ralph W. Tyler, "Can Intelligence Tests Be used to Predict Educability," in Kenneth Eells, *et al., Intelligence and Cultural Differences,* (Chicago: University of Chicago Press, 1951), p. 43.

[15] Donald Hebb, a leading psychologist, makes the assumption that the early childhood period is of decisive importance in determining later intelligence. He believes that Negro and poor white children have had insufficient stimulation in their early development, and that this accounts for their lower *functioning* intelligence at a later age. He accepts the intelligence test performance as an accurate indicator of operating intelligence although he believes it to be a completely inaccurate index of *capacity*—inherent intelligence. See Donald O. Hebb, *Organization of Behavior,* (New York: John Wiley & Sons, 1949), Chapter II.

extremely far-fetched because, whatever one may say about the environment of these children, it certainly is not lacking in stimulation per se. Witness the crowded homes and streets, the noise, parties, TV sets, the sports, games, fights, etc.

2. Moreover, the family life includes a good deal of sibling interaction, physical punishment, definite toilet training, masturbation inhibition, breast feeding, and various responsibility demands. Regardless of the particular evaluation one may wish to place on these practices, they do appear to provide stimulation. This environment seems quite distinct from that of children reared in isolation from society.

3. Haggard's findings further call into question the inference concerning "basic retardation," because if the I.Q. can be so markedly improved by only three hours of special training, surely the childhood experiences cannot have been so limiting or irreversible. It might also be added that much of the behavior of deprived children, in non-academic spheres, gives evidence of considerable spontaneity, a trait not ordinarily associated with a history of deficient stimulation.

Creativity and the I.Q.

Erich Fromm comments on intelligence tests that "they measure not so much the capacity for reason and understanding as the capacity for quick mental adaptation to a given situation; 'mental adjustment tests' would be the adequate name for them."[16]

The items used on the tests do not require any intrinsic interest or curiosity on the part of the subject. On the contrary, if he becomes too interested in any one item he will probably take too much time on it and possibly give an unconventional response that might be marked as being wrong. The motivation called for on the test is not interest in the specific questions as such, but rather an overall competitive motivation to do well. But the intelligence of certain kinds of people may not really be tapped unless they are deeply involved in the specific problem on which they are working. This is more likely to be the case with disadvantaged individuals.

Psychologists have come to disagree with the notion that a

[16] *Man For Himself*, ⟨New York: Rinehart, 1947, p. 75⟩.

high I.Q. is the mark of "giftedness" or creativity. Dr. Westcott[17] at Vassar College has developed a specific test for measuring creativity that has been validated in terms of actual creative accomplishments of the students—accomplishments such as writing a piece of music, poetry, and the like. He finds little relationship between creativity and I.Q. scores.[18]

The I.Q. of deprived individuals is generally relatively low but their creativity is often shown in non-academic ways: A prominent labor union economist, Solomon Barkin, Research Director of the Textile Workers' Union of America, has said that he has seen a number of wage incentive schemes that seemed to him foolproof, with no way of adapting them so that they would benefit the workers. But he has never seen a plan that in practice could not be adapted or "jimmied" in their favor. He reports that a number of times he had objected to management proposals for incentive plans as unfavorable to the workers, only to be told by the men involved, "Don't worry, we'll figure out how to jimmy it." He, himself, could not see any possibility for

[17] Malcolm R. Westcott, "A Method for the Study of Creativity as a Special Case of Problem Solving," paper presented at the Eastern Psychological Association, New York City, April 16, 1960.

[18] An article in *The New York Times* (February 18, 1961, p. 40) reports an important summary made by Professor Calvin W. Taylor, of Utah, concerning the relationship of I.Q. to creativity:

"He cites experiments at various places in the country that have shown that if an I.Q. test is used to select top level talent, about 70 per cent of those who have the highest 20 per cent of the scores on a creativity test battery will be missed.

"Traditional intelligence tests, he says, cover only a very few of the fifty or more dimensions of the mind that have been discovered.

"He tells of a test in which the researchers selected twenty-eight dimensions of the mind they felt were relevant to success in a job in the physical sciences. Scientists then were asked to arrange those characteristics in order of rank in terms of importance to the job.

" 'Traditional intelligence tests have included about five or six of these characteristics, such as general reasoning, vocabulary ability, number ability, memory for ideas, ability to visualize spatially and, perhaps, perceptual speed,' he comments.

" 'All but one of these traditional intelligence factors ranked below twentieth in the list.'

"That is, nineteen out of the twenty characteristics considered by scientists most important on the job in science were not included in the traditional I.Q. tests. Examples of these top characteristics were intellectual flexibilities, fluencies, originality, penetration, redefinition ability, and sensitivity to problems."

manipulation of the scheme, yet in every case, within a year, the men in the shop had been able to figure out ways of "beating the system" that he, an expert, could not envision. We are not discussing the ethics of the actions, but the creativity manifested.

We have frequently observed children in deprived neighborhoods playing basketball by tying a fruit basket, with the bottom removed, to a fire escape. This requires a fair amount of creative ingenuity.

Action Implications

As a result of the re-evaluation of the standard I.Q. tests and their particular limitations for underprivileged children, a number of recommendations have come forth:

1. One suggestion is to employ performance tests wherever possible, since these appear to be less affected by the vocabulary limitations of the deprived child. Unfortunately, while these tests have a number of advantages, their use does not overcome the problems of rapport, motivation, and test-taking skill encountered with underprivileged youngsters.

2. Davis and Eels have developed a "culture fair" games test which in many ways seems more appropriate for underprivileged groups. While some deprived individuals fare better on this test, others do not. The problems of rapport, motivation, and practice appear here again, although the motivation problem is partially reduced by making the test a game.

3. Murray and others have suggested that the deficiencies of the standard I.Q. tests be corrected. He feels that the tests are potentially valuable tools, and rejects the argument advanced by some that they should be discarded because of their weaknesses. Not only can the tests be improved, but different dimensions of intelligence can be tapped. Items employed need not be brief; tasks showing no change with age can be utilized; time limits may be removed or lengthened; less academic, bookish problems can be employed; the thinking involved in solving the problems can be evaluated along with the accuracy of the final answer; items that discriminate between deprived and middle-class groups can be removed from the tests, just as items dis-

criminating between the sexes are removed in test construction;[19] emotionally loaded items can be selected and the responses to them compared with the more value-free items. These are just a few of the possible changes that might be introduced to strengthen the tests.

4. Haggard's study, in which the measured I.Q. of deprived children was raised considerably with only three hours of special training, highlights the need for giving these children directed practice, and developing new test-taking habits. Deprived children are less test conscious and are not accustomed to being evaluated. They have poor auditory habits, do not concentrate sufficiently on the examiner's instructions, do not pick up the examinations readily, and, in general, are lethargic, apathetic, and ill at ease in the test situation. Sometimes they hurry through the test, just to get it over with and to remove themselves from the situation. Some deprived children are more serious about the test, but they are usually over-cautious, anxious and slow.

Simple, undirected practice in test-taking will not overcome these difficulties. In the course of their school careers, deprived youngsters receive much practice, but it is unmotivated, meaningless practice. Experience is a good teacher only when one knows what to learn from it; by itself, practice can merely reinforce bad habits.

5. Haggard's research also demonstrates the great need for rapport. Haggard trained his examiners so that they would know how to work with deprived youngsters. This kind of training is decisive for clinicians and teachers. The clinician has to know how to elicit questions from the deprived child, and how to provide answers in terms that are clearly understood, are repeated often, with numerous examples. He must realize that simply giving the child the test instructions, and having him nod that they are understood, is by no means any guarantee. Deprived children, unless they are at ease with the examiner, are much more likely to be passive in the test situation.

Rapport is also dependent upon the examiner having confidence that the child *can* do well. In a sense, the clinician has to convey

---

[19] It is fairly typical in I.Q. test construction either to retain only the items which do not show a sex difference statistically, or to balance the items so that each sex is favored equally.

to the deprived child that he understands why the child has not done well in the past, but that now the conditions are different and the child will therefore be able to show his real ability. This should not be false or artificial; in fact, the examiner should believe this and let the child perceive his optimistic, but not demanding or pressing, expectation.

6. The teacher might choose to ignore the standard I.Q. results because of the limitations of the test, and instead attempt to discover the "hidden I.Q." of the deprived child. This can best be done by noting the child's contributions in discussing a topic which interests him a good deal, such as popular music or the world series. Role-playing (acting out situations) and physical tasks in general are useful for estimating his potential intelligence.

A good deal of the behavior of underprivileged individuals outside the school context indicates considerable intelligence in terms of dealing with problems and interests close to their own lives. Their intelligence is more fully shown in games such as dominoes, in sports, in humor, and in gossip. They are often surprisingly perceptive in sensing various subtle forms of discrimination and the children demonstrate much misdirected ingenuity in avoiding truant officers and the law. In general, it might be said that they are rather "human smart," and their "hidden I.Q.'s" are best seem in their human relations.

vii

THE SLOW GIFTED CHILD

It is often contended that deprived children are non-verbal, that they think in a slow, inadequate manner, and cannot conceptualize. While there are elements of truth in this portrayal, we think that it is a somewhat distorted picture, particularly in the invidious interpretation given the "elements."

How do deprived children learn and think? What are the characteristics of their so-called "cognitive style?" Do they have any creative potential? These are questions to which educators must give serious attention.

Poor or Slow?

An interesting confusion prevails in education circles between the "poor learner" and the "slow learner." The two are assumed to be identical. But need this be so? In a pragmatic culture such as ours, oriented toward quantity, speed, and measurement, this error can be fallen into readily. In the classroom it is terribly easy to believe that the child who learns the lesson quickly is a better learner than one who takes a long period of time. And sometimes this is the correct conclusion, as in reading, where studies show that faster readers understand better what they have read. The same thing appears to be true with regard to learning subject matter, such as history or geography. But here the problem is more complicated. The child who learns history more slowly is likely to be ignored and, unwittingly, discouraged by the teacher. Even if she does not ignore him but, on the contrary, gives him special attention, she may reflect to him her implicit assumption that he is a poor student. She may demand less of him, for example. The point is that she never sees the slowness as simply another style of learning with potential strengths of its own; nor does she see potential weaknesses (not *necessary* weaknesses) in the fast learner, who may become glib or impatient with tasks requiring protracted attention. *Because of the treatment he receives in the school system, the slow learner then may become the poor learner.*

It is time to put an end to the negative description of the term "slow" in the learning process. Slowness can reflect many things. It can indicate caution, a desire to be very thorough, great interest that may constrain against rushing through a problem, or a meticulous style. Or it may indicate a desire to mull things over, an emphasis on the concrete and physical. It may also indicate intellectual inadequacy. Extreme slowness probably does connote inadequacy in the absence of counter-indications. Even here we have to be very careful to check all possible blocks, not only the obvious emotional disturbances. There may be many other types of blockage as well, such as auditory blocks, reading difficulties (not of emotional origin), antagonism to the teacher, etc.

The nature of the slowness itself also has to be carefully examined. A delayed end product does not necessarily mean a slow process of thinking. Because a child takes a long time to arrive at an answer does not mean that his thinking is retarded. It may be that his thinking is more circuitous, that he is easily distracted, that he will not venture an answer until he is certain; and there is a host of other possibilities.

While our culture emphasizes speed, there is really no reason to assume that gifted, creative people have to learn rapidly or perform rapidly. Some people take a long time to learn basic concepts, but when they finally do so, they may use these ideas in a thoughtful, penetrating fashion. Others may learn a concept rapidly and then switch to some other area without ever pursuing the concept in depth. There are many slow people who only demonstrate their intellectual power on tasks in which it takes them a long time to get interested, and which have no time requirements. We have seen a fairly large number of college students whose grades and I.Q. scores were low, but who performed quite brilliantly on particular problems or in subjects in which they were deeply immersed. Their poor averages were simply a reflection of the pace required in college that is not attuned to their own style of work. They often fail courses where they could do extremely well if given more time. Actually, an extended college program, say, of five years, would benefit these students immeasurably. Educators tend to think of shortening college to three years for students who supposedly do not require the usual four years. But is there any reason why college could not be lengthened for these students who have a different style and pace of work? Many of these youngsters do, in fact, attend college for five or more years because they have to go to summer school to make up the courses they fail when carrying a schedule that is too heavy for them.

There is little doubt that the deprived child typically works on academic problems in a slower manner. This is shown in many different ways: he requires more examples before seeing a point, arriving at a conclusion, or forming a concept. He is unwilling to jump to conclusions or to generalize quickly (exceptions to the rule bother him). He is a slower reader, slower problem solver, slower at getting down to work, slower in taking tests.

It is important to note that in many areas of life the underprivileged individual is not at all slow; quite the contrary, he is frequently remarkably quick. By way of illustration, in athletic activities and many games he functions rapidly and seems to think quickly. He seems to be both perceptive and quick in judging expressions on people's faces. When verbalizing in his own idiom, he does not appear to be sluggish at all. In figuring out ways of "beating the system" in the factory he is often astoundingly fast. These observations suggest that part of his slowness in the academic sphere is probably due to unfamiliarity with the subjects, limitations with formal language, and insecurity in this setting. But these "defensive" reasons for cautious slowness do not tell the whole story either. It appears at first glance that in the more direct sensory and physical areas, the deprived individual can be fast and acute, while in the middle-class settings in which he is unsure, slow caution prevails. The problem gets much more complex, however, once we begin to notice that there are a great many physical activities in which the deprived are notably slow. We had the opportunity of observing over a long period of time a highly skilled mechanic who came from a deprived background. Whenever he built anything in his house such as a cellar or a table, he did so in a meticulous fashion; likewise, when he worked on his car. He seemed to like to work in this manner, mulling things over, taking his time. Most old-time skilled workers like a leisurely pace. The shoemaker does not rush through his work, as a rule, but tends to do it carefully, patiently, at a moderate clip. This is often connected with pride in the product produced. Apparently, then, in things that are taken very seriously, things of deep concern, matters of personal pride, the slow style takes over. Workmanship is not a game or a party, but something enduring. It is also likely that many of the off-the-job pursuits of people like our mechanic—who, incidentally, likes to fish as well as to build furniture—are a reaction against the fast pace of modern industry.

Another source of the slow pace, which is not a sign of inadequacy or insecurity, may lie in the physical, less world-centered approach of the deprived person. It is not as easy to get into a problem or to cope with it as quickly if one has to go through all the steps physically. A word-oriented person can deal with most academic problems facilely, albeit sometimes glibly. A physical individual, on the other hand, likes to *do* as much as he can in thinking through a problem. This is often time-consuming.

While there are various special classes for slow learners, these classes do not really aim at developing advanced conceptual skills. They assume that the slow learner's ability is basically limited, rather than recognizing that he has a different style of learning that may have positive attributes. They do not envision any potentially gifted children among the slow learners.

Do and See vs. Talk and Hear

In Chapter IV, the physical or motoric style of deprived groups was noted. This style is evidenced in a number of familiar ways:

1. They often appear to do better on performance tests of intelligence.
2. They like to draw.
3. Role-playing is an attractive technique to them.
4. They often use their fingers when counting, and move their lips when reading.
5. They like to participate in sports.
6. They employ physical forms of discipline.
7. They appear to think in spatial terms rather than temporal terms (they often have poor time perspective).

While their more limited temporal perspective undoubtedly produces difficulties, the spatial focus has a positive side to it. Spatial conceptualization permits an entire problem to be seen at once—it does not have temporal restrictions.[1]

The physical learner is, as was noted earlier, usually a slower learner, particularly in the early stages. But it is quite likely that he achieves a different kind of understanding of a problem than the faster, symbolic learner. Unfortunately, because our school system rewards speed, physical learners are discouraged and do not develop, while the symbolic learner is encouraged and moves forward.

While the deprived child does not easily get into problems, and has a short attention span, once he does become involved he is often able to work tenaciously for long stretches at a time. This may be a characteristic of the physical learner, because in order for him to learn he needs to have more of his whole body responding, and this requires a longer "warm-up" period. We are reminded here of the warming-up required in role-playing, which is more "physical." Highly verbal people, who, incidentally, often resist role-playing or function in it in a highly intellectual manner, seem to need much less of a warm-up period in studying. Since they use their "muscles" less in thinking, this is perhaps comprehensible.

How Deep is the Physical Approach?

It is interesting to note that the deprived child's motoric style or approach may not actually be as imbedded as might appear at first glance. There is the possibility that the difference in approach is

[1] This positive aspect of spatial conceptualization was suggested by Irving Taylor in a personal communication.

more of a set which is capable of manipulation and change under certain circumstances. This interpretation is suggested by a finding of Miller and Swanson.[2] On one of the tests (the Carl Hollow Square Test) employed to determine whether people tended to be "conceptual" or "motoric," the researchers wanted to see if their subjects could switch their orientations if the instructions were altered slightly. That is, could a physical person perform in a conceptual fashion and vice versa. Miller and Swanson used two sets of instructions. One encouraged the subjects to take a conceptual approach: ". . . it helps to work these problems if you spend some time trying to figure out what is the best way to do them. . . ." Another set of instructions encouraged the subjects to be motoric: ". . . you can solve the problem better by trying all the possible ways to fit these together that you can in the time allowed. . . ." Under these conditions both groups were able to use styles that were not characteristic of them. *Deprived children could perform conceptually about as well as the non-deprived groups.*[3] This is one more example of their hidden intelligence. It is also further evidence that the early environment of the deprived child has not produced irreversible effects.

The Concrete and the Abstract

Abstract thinking is ultimately rooted in concrete sensory phenomena. But most of us in the course of educational experience have come to appreciate abstractions for their own sake. This is true whether we are talking about scientific theories or artistic—literary productions. We do not have to see the concrete applications or origins of Shakespeare in order to appreciate

[2] Daniel R. Miller and Guy E. Swanson, *Inner Conflict and Defense,* (New York: Henry Holt, 1960), p. 346.

[3] Siller found that low-status children do more poorly than high-status children on a variety of tests of conceptual ability and that they are less adequate in handling abstract concepts. In light of Miller and Swanson's findings, there is the possibility that this is due more to a "set" than a basic ability. An interesting residual finding of Siller's is that the differences between the high and low status groups is due to a small number of especially "low scorers" in the deprived groups. "When the groups were examined with these subjects removed, there were no significant status differences." See Jerome Siller, "Socioeconomic Status and Conceptual Thinking," *Journal of Abnormal and Social Psychology,* November, 1957, p. 365–371.

him. But deprived children have a very different attitude toward abstract concepts. They need to have the abstract constantly and intimately pinned to the immediate, the sensory, the topical. This is not to say that they dislike abstract thinking. It is, rather, that they do it differently. Moreover, after they have acquired some feeling for broad generalizations from seeing their derivation and application in practice, then the deprived individual may, to some degree, begin to appreciate abstract formulations per se. This probably comes at a later stage of development, and possibly even then the abstractions will be more firmly connected to things that can be seen, felt, and acted upon.

Since the deprived child approaches abstractions from the concrete, the immediate, the teacher must do likewise. The following is a vivid illustration reported to us recently by a junior high school teacher:[4]

"On the day before the following lesson, the teacher told the class the story of Caliban from Shakespeare's *The Tempest*. The next day, the class walked into a darkened classroom and the teacher, walking around the room and reading by a flickering flashlight, recited the poem by Louis Untermeyer called 'Caliban in the Coal Mines.' It is a plaintive, almost sacrilegious, appeal to the Lord for better conditions in the mines: 'God, if You wish for our love, Fling us a handful of stars.' The lights in the classroom were turned on near the ending of this last line of the poem. Allowing the class to come out of its trance slowly, the teacher distributed copies of the poem and requested, and received, acceptable meanings to certain words. In the discussion that followed the teacher asked why the poet had called his miner Caliban. The answer supplied by a thirteen-year-old girl was: 'They were both in the dark.'"

This same teacher states further:[5]

"Announce a lesson in 'literature'—especially one in poetry— and you will receive an assortment of groans. Announce that you will tell the class a story and you will receive respectful but reserved expectancy. State further that this is the story of two sets of parents who, because of their unwillingness to adapt to the

[4] Personal communication from Harold Kirsch, a New York City Junior High School teacher.
[5] *Ibid.*

present time, contributed to the destruction of their own children. You will have your audience in the palm of your hand. On the basis of a sympathetic, even empathic approach to the point of view of the adolescent, you have motivated the class to the study of Shakespeare's *Romeo and Juliet*. Will deprived children respond to these techniques? Having used them in my classes, I shall vouch that arguments have started because somebody said that Juliet was a fool to destroy herself for a man. Somebody else wondered if we sometimes learn the truth too late (speaking of the elder Montagues and Capulets). It is not difficult to direct such thinking into the value of having a mind stretched by study-ing and observing and learning."

The Outside vs. The Inside

Deprived children for the most part are not introspective or introverted; nor are they greatly concerned with the self. They respond much more to the external, to the outside. They are not given to self-blame or self-criticism, but rather are more likely to see the causes of their problems in external forces. Sometimes this can take the form of scapegoating and projection, but it may also lead to appropriate placement of censure and accompanying anger.

That they are not introspective in focus does not mean that they are incapable of inner thought, imagination, and feeling. But rather, again, as in the case of the concrete and the abstract— the external stimulation must precede the inner development. They are not given to direct enjoyment of introspection qua introspection, but instead require, at least at first, that it be stimulated by external sources.

The Games Format

Anyone who has worked with deprived children knows that one of the surest ways to involve them in an activity is to make it into a game. Now, this is true of all children to some extent, but it is especially true of the underprivileged. Davis and Eells have capitalized on this idea by developing an intelligence test in the form of a game. Cartoon-like personality tests such as the Rosenzweig Picture Frustration Test are much more appealing to underprivileged individuals.

Teachers have told about setting up a mock court in the classroom which enabled the class to discuss discipline, justice, and government in a meaningful way. Originally they had found it difficult to interest the deprived children in these subjects, but the excitement of a make-believe court attracted considerable attention and provided a good beginning for discussion on a higher, more abstract level.

One of the reasons why the new teaching machines are likely to appeal to the deprived child is that they operate pretty much like games. In this connection, we are reminded of the exciting work of O. K. Moore at Yale, where, by using special mechanical devices constructed in the form of games, he has been able to teach three-year-old children to read, write, and type.[6] The use of machines of this kind on a pre-school level with deprived children holds great promise. Perhaps even more important could be their use in special classes for "retarded" children. These game-like devices might enable these children to catch up rapidly and return to the main educational "track," and thus reduce the present "two track" character of the educational system.

What is the source of the "games" orientation of the deprived? Apparently, it is related to their down-to-earth, spontaneous approach to things. Their extra-verbal communication (motoric, visual) is usually called forth in games, most of which are not word-bound. Also, most games (not all, by any means), are person-centered and generally are concerned with direct action and visible results. Games are usually sharply defined and structured, with clear-cut goals. The rules are definite and can be readily absorbed. The deprived child enjoys the challenge of the game and feels he can "do" it; this is in sharp contrast to many verbal tasks.

[6] The effectiveness of the teaching machines ultimately has to be evaluated in the framework of the long-range learning sets produced by such devices. The present hue and cry concerning their apparent effectiveness has to be weighed in relation to the attitudes toward learning and thinking which eventuate. Also, much of their observed effectiveness may be due to a "gimmick" or novelty (placebo) effect, and not to the intrinsic learning principles presumably involved. Moore's work with small children would not seem to be subject to this effect, but the long-term effects on the child's attitudes toward learning will have to be appraised carefully. See *Time Magazine*, November 7, 1960, p. 103, for a brief presentation of O. K. Moore's methods.

Why Does the Progressive Approach Fail?

Progressive education emphasizes "learning by doing." This fits in with the physical approach of the deprived child. Progressive education emphasizes concrete, experience-centered learning, attuned to the pace of the child. This is exactly what the deprived child needs so much. Why, then, does the progressive approach appear to fail with these children—why do they find it so unappealing on the whole? This is a puzzling problem. Certainly, it must be said, there are a fair number of progressive-minded teachers who, in stressing vivid, example-centered lessons, have been successful with deprived children. But on the average, it is the old-style, strict, highly structured teacher who appears to be most popular and effective with underprivileged children. When this teacher is also lively, and builds concepts from the ground up, and makes an effort to "win the children to learning," she is the model teacher for these youngsters.

The progressive approach by itself, however, does not catch on. It has too many features that are essentially alien to the culture of the deprived: the permissiveness; the accent on self—the internal—the introspective; creativity and growth as central goals of education; the stress on play; the underestimation of discipline and authority. All these values are contradictory to the traditional attitudes and personality characteristics of the deprived.

What is needed is a perfect marriage of the traditional and the progressive. The traditionalist contributes structure, rules, discipline, authority, rote, order, organization, and strong external demands for achievement. He fights to win the child to a high level of conceptual learning. The progressivist places the emphasis on the importance of motivation; the down-to-earth learning by doing; examples drawn from the experience of the child—beginning in the present and moving toward the broad, the abstract, the cultural heritage.

This is the combination that can break through the block which separates the child and the school.

A Different Wave Length

In summary, then, it can be said that the following characteristics are fairly typical of the deprived child's style:

1. Physical and visual rather than aural.
2. Content-centered rather than form-centered.
3. Externally oriented rather than introspective.
4. Problem-centered rather than abstract-centered.
5. Inductive rather than deductive.
6. Spatial rather than temporal.
7. Slow, careful, patient, persevering (in areas of importance), rather than quick, clever, facile, flexible.

It can readily be seen that many of these characteristics overlap. They seem to form a pattern that, according to Irving Taylor, is very similar to that found among one type of highly creative person.[7] Why then does the potential creativity of the underprivileged child fail to materialize? There are a number of reasons, but perhaps the most important is his verbal difficulties. The following chapter is directly concerned with this problem.

[7] Personal communication from Irving Taylor.

viii

The greatest block to the realization of the deprived individual's creative potential appears to be his verbal inadequacies. He seems to have enormous difficulty expressing himself verbally in many situations. For example, when interviewing underprivileged individuals one of the most characteristic comments encountered is "You know what I mean." It is liberally appended to all kinds of answers and occurs even when the respondent is at ease with the interviewer. This difficulty of expression also takes place in the school; consequently, there has arisen a rather firm belief that the deprived child is basically inarticulate.

While it would be easy enough to conclude that the underprivileged are essentially non-verbal, careful examination indicates that the problem is not nearly so simple. Because verbal ability is so important, it is necessary to try to specify the exact nature of the deprived individual's verbal functioning, rather than simply to assume that he is non-verbal or less verbal.

The Nature of the Verbal Deficit

Eells and Havighurst[1] point out that deprived children use a great many words with a fair amount of precision, but these are not the words used in the school. Success in school is based

[1] Kenneth Eells *et al., Intelligence and Cultural Differences* (Chicago: University of Chicago Press, 1951), p. 43.

on facility with a middle-class vocabulary, not with the language of the underprivileged.

What then is the vocabulary pattern of the deprived? Basil Bernstein, the British sociologist, believes that deprived groups are at home with what he calls "public language," but are deficient in "formal language." Public, or informal, language is characterized by "short, grammatically simple, often unfinished sentences . . . simple and repetitive use of conjunctions (so, then, and, because); frequent use of short commands and questions, etc."[2]

Walter Murray reminds us that in everyday conversation deprived individuals demonstrate a language that is often rich in simile and analogy.[3] This is seen in their use of slang and in cursing. A large proportion of the new words that have become part of our language (e.g., *oomph*) are said to have had their origins among deprived groups. Some of the words come in via musicians, while others come in through the hipsters and the Beatniks who have been much influenced by the culture of the underprivileged. Newspapers like the *New York Daily News* also reflect some of this vivid, abbreviated language. The communication of the deprived is famous for its use of imaginative nicknames and shortenings—the British "never-never" for installment buying, "telly" for TV, "pub" for bar or public place.

The inventive word power of the deprived is also shown in the language of the gang:

bop—to fight
bread—money
cool it—take it easy
dig—to understand
jazz—worthless talk
pad—room
rank—to insult

[2] By contrast, some characteristics of formal language are: "Accurate order and syntax regulate what is said; and logical modifications and stress are mediated through a gramatically complex sentence construction, especially through the use of a range of conjunctions and relative clauses. Frequent use of prepositions which indicate logical relationships as well as prepositions which indicate temporal and spatial contiguity; frequent use of impersonal pronouns, 'it,' 'one,' etc." See Basil Bernstein, "A Public Language," *British Journal of Sociology*, December, 1959, pp. 311–323.

[3] Personal communication from Walter Murray.

pecks—food
snake—spy
sound—talk

The Institute for Developmental Studies, under Martin Deutsch, is currently conducting a series of investigations of the language patterns of deprived children. Preliminary findings, while not conclusive, are suggestive:

> In our own study, we have already encountered interesting surprises. We assumed that the lower-class child, when confronted with a word-association task, will respond in a somewhat stereotyped or rigid manner; instead we find that both first and fifth grade lower-class children give rich associations that sometimes lack logical continuity. Example: to the stimulus word 'home,' one of our subjects associated, 'well, living with your mother and father, and taking care of it so the ceilings won't fall down, just like my house almost the whole ceiling is falling down. If you want a good home, you have to get all the furniture that belongs in the home.' Thus, it is possible that the oft-stated conclusion on the verbal impoverishment of the child from the culturally deprived home is most striking when he is presented with highly structured tasks, and that verbal enrichment techniques, which take advantage of his freer flow of language in more unstructured situations, may help him to meet his language and scholastic potential.[4]

Deutsch's staff utilizes a novel technique to elicit the child's "spontaneous language," which in the case of the deprived child seems to be more developed than might be expected. The child is presented with a large toy clown; the clown's nose lights up when the child talks, and the child is free to choose his topic, or even to repeat himself; the clown's nose fails to light up when the child is silent, and the child is told this means "the clown is sad." Deprived children are much more verbally expressive in this situation.[5]

Other findings reported by the Institute are:

1. Deprived children appear to be poor in the use of verbs, but much better with descriptive adjectives.

2. Deprived children seem to understand more language than

---

[4] Mimeographed report from the Institute for Developmental Studies, Department of Psychiatry, New York Medical College.
[5] *Ibid.*

they speak (their "receptive" linguistic ability is much better than their "expressive" language).

3. Deprived children demonstrate a surprising ability for phantasy (as seen in the clown situation).

4. Deprived children express themselves best in spontaneous, unstructured situations.[6]

In role-playing sessions we have had occasion to observe that the verbal performance of deprived children is markedly improved in the discussion period following the session. When talking about some *action* they have *seen*, deprived children are apparently able to verbalize much more fully. Typically they *do not verbalize well in response to words alone.* They express themselves more readily when reacting to things they can see and do. Words as stimuli are not sufficient for them as a rule. Ask a juvenile delinquent who comes from a disadvantaged background what he doesn't like about school or the teacher and you will get an abbreviated, inarticulate reply. But have a group of these youngsters act out a school scene in which someone plays the teacher, and you will discover a stream of verbal consciousness that is almost impossible to shut off.

Words and Creativity

Irving Taylor, formerly Project Coordinator on the staff of the Institute for Developmental Studies, has some novel ideas about untapped creative potential in disadvantaged children. He believes that these children are not nearly so non-verbal as is generally thought. He says that they use words in a different way and are not as dependent on words for their sole form of communication, but that nevertheless they are imaginative at the verbal level.[7]

Taylor finds on word association tests that deprived children give responses that are often less conventional, more unusual, original, and independent. They seem to be more flexible and visual with language. For example, to the word "stone," deprived children are more willing to give associations such as "solid" and "hard," responses that encompass the perceptual qualities of the object. They are also more likely to say "throw it in a lake,"

[6] *Ibid.*
[7] Personal communication from Irving Taylor.

"chop things up with it." Non-deprived children restrict their associations more to standard synonyms like "rock," "pebbles." The deprived child includes these words also—he know that they "belong" with "stone"—but he is freer in including other words.[8]

Taylor feels that deprived individuals are not as restricted by verbal forms of communication, but tend to permit language to interact more with non-verbal means of communication, such as gestures and pictures. This interaction with other kinds of communication gives them the potential for "breaking through the language barrier"; they are not forced to think in terms of the structure of language as are so many people. *They are less word-bound.*

Taylor believes that their wide range of associations indicates a freer use of language, which may be an important attribute of one type of creativity. He contends that not only do studies of creative people indicate that they have greater "semantic flexibility," but also that they respond well to visual, tactile, and kinesthetic cues. In general, their non-aural senses seem to be especially acute. Taylor notes that this pattern resembles the mental approach of the underprivileged child in many respects.

Finally, Taylor points out that when the creative potential of deprived children remains educationally untapped, there is a much greater possibility of its finding outlets in delinquency and destructive behavior.[9]

One-Track Creativity

While creativity too often goes unstimulated in the school milieu, one brand of it is, at least, indirectly encouraged. This is the kind of creativity that is called forth by our best examinations when they require the bringing together of ideas from

[8] Taylor recognizes the possibility that the wide range of associations of deprived children may simply reflect a laxity or looseness with language; in other words, they may have many different associations because they do not know the meaning of words. He tested this alternative interpretation with a carefully constructed, Thurstone-type, ordinal word-distance scale, in which the children are asked to select from a large list the words which "go with" the original stimulus word and the words which do not belong with it. Preliminary results appear to support the thesis that deprived children do know the meanings of the words, but have a wider range of associations. They do not include words at random that are inappropriate.

[9] Personal communication from Irving Taylor.

many sources in order to answer the test question. At its best, this demand does stimulate the reorganization of concepts—an important type of creativity, perhaps best described as "convergent creativity."[10] But there is another kind of creativity, less apt to be sanctioned in the grade-dominated school, and more likely to be encountered in the slow gifted child. Here the individual relentlessly pursues one line of thought, one problem, one search, one thread—sometimes for years. This person has "one-track creativity."[11] He may ignore many areas of learning, and thus there are important gaps in his knowledge. When such a person's ability is perceived—and this is not usually the case— it is described as "uneven brilliance." The unevenness is often costly—on examinations, interviews, and the like. It is a style that has escaped the bureaucratization of creativity, and because of this often goes unrecognized and undeveloped.

Creative people are generally thought to be flexible and open-minded. This is certainly true of one kind of creative person (the convergent type). But the one-track individual often fixedly absorbs everything pertaining to his scheme or problem, and is not at all interested in other points of view. This person may be difficult to get along with personally, but he is nonetheless talented.

In a fascinating article concerned with a strategy for the development of talent, Dael Wolfle,[12] editor of *Science*, argues that our entire testing system favors the broad, well-rounded student, and overlooks the student with special abilities whose overall scores are not high.

There is a substantial need for more single-minded creativity. It is our belief that this kind of creativity will be found among deprived individuals who, as we have remarked earlier, often possess a rigid tenacity once they have overcome the initial barrier of disinterest. But, of course, this form of creativity is found among different social groups, and the points made have wider relevance than to the underprivileged alone.

[10] This type of creativity is similar to what J. P. Guilford describes as the "convergent" type.

[11] This kind of creative person is similar in some respects to Guilford's "divergent" type who is characterized by much searching about, going off in various directions.

[12] Dael Wolfle, "Diversity of Talent," *The American Psychologist*, August, 1960, pp. 535–545.

The Achilles Heel

Despite various sources of latent creativity, underprivileged children apparently do not realize their potential because of formal language deficiencies. This is their Achilles heel.

Nevertheless, these children have considerable facility with informal or public language, and this is expressed best in unstructured, spontaneous situations; they verbalize more freely around action and things they can see; they understand more language than they speak; their non-verbal forms of expression are more highly developed; and they often have imaginative associations to words.

The forms of communication characteristic of deprived children raise important educational questions. The acquisition of knowledge obviously requires some degree of facility with *formal* language. As we have seen, underprivileged children are capable of utilizing language in a rich and free fashion, have well-developed, non-verbal ways of communicating, but are sorely lacking in advanced linguistic form. The problem is how to help them to attain this level of language so that their creative potential can be realized. It would be easy to say, as many have said, that we must give these children what middle-class parents give their children—we must stimulate them in the use of language through reading, discussion, and the like. However, it is probable that this would not work nor would it make the best use of the deprived child's particular mode of functioning. It would seem that he has to be taught in a different way, with the aim of giving him the necessary linguistic techniques without having him become word-bound. His non-linguistic skills should not be ignored or suppressed, but rather brought out and integrated with verbal communication. Thus, it would seem essential that the method of teaching formal language to deprived children take advantage of their communication style by employing teaching techniques that stress the visual, the physical, the active, as much as possible. We must be careful not to try to make these children over into replicas of middle-class children. The educational system should be pluralistic enough, broad enough, to find a place for a variety of mental styles.

ix

THE EFFECTIVE TEACHER

Teaching deprived children does not consist of gimmicks or tricks. Much more decisive are certain basic attitudes. Effective teachers use different techniques—there is not just one right approach, although there are many *wrong* approaches. For example, toughness and brutality are most ineffective. Perhaps the best overall principle is to be *consistent*. These children want a teacher on whom they can depend. If she tells them to stop chewing gum one day, she can not permit them to do it the next.

Let us list some general characteristics and behavior patterns that appear desirable. The teacher should be straight-forward, direct, and should clearly define what is to be done as much as possible. At the same time she should be informal, warm, down-to-earth. Snobbishness and indirection are major pitfalls. So is cynicism, although naïveté is equally dangerous.

A female teacher can be somewhat maternal and express a degree of physical affection, but she must avoid gushing. The pattern displayed by the nuns in parochial schools is often well responded to. The Sisters appear to be quiet, sincere, and evidence physical warmth in a simple, dignified fashion without overdoing it.

The Value Problem

The teacher should recognize the special "value problem" she faces in a culturally deprived setting. Her own values are likely to be different from those of her pupils. This may not always be true because, to some extent, basic American values are held, if with different emphasis, by all people who have grown up in our society. However, as we have seen, the mores of the disadvantaged are in many respects different from those of the traditional middle-class person. Even if the teacher herself comes from a deprived background, her present situation in life has undoubtedly produced a new frame of reference. In this general context there are a number of alternatives open to her. She can concentrate on those values which she holds in common with the pupils and ignore the differences. This is not always easy to do. She can try to ignore value questions entirely and focus on teaching basic skills and knowledge. If the deprived group desires education mainly for vocational improvement, she can furnish the information needed and attempt to by-pass value problems. Again, this is not easy because values creep in unconsciously, although it may be a useful goal for which to strive. There is one more option, and this viewpoint underlies the present book. The teacher may, in a designated area, explicitly and openly disagree with a value bias like anti-intellectualism. If she does this directly and honestly, not snobbishly or manipulatively, she may be able to sway students, and may also be more at ease in her relationship to them. After all, we are often ill at ease with people, not necessarily when we disagree with them, but when we cannot talk about the disagreement. Of course, disagreement, to be fruitful, has to take place within a framework of general acceptance, and so the teacher, in order to be effective in opposing certain beliefs, has to be able to share, or at least respect, other sentiments.

Breaking Through the Cultural Barrier

The problem of achieving classroom rapport is a difficult one. The teacher must be prepared for the likelihood that the children will not accept her initially; in fact, they may be downright hostile. They will probably test her just as gangs test social workers, and she will have to prove herself in a number of ways. She will have to prove that she does not look down her nose at them, that she is not afraid of them, that she is not disgusted, and that she is not naive or foolish or "soft." In a sense she is made responsible for, and has to live down, all the earlier difficulties these children have come up against in the school system and, to some extent, in society at large. She has to expect a difficult transition period at first, and she must lean over backwards not to get rattled or disillusioned. Actually, if she can hurdle the initial barrier and begin to build a favorable relationship to the class, she may be surprised at how rapidly things begin to move. For once she is perceived as their friend—on their side, so to speak—the whole classroom situation will take on a new character, and learning may progress smoothly. What she has to guard against firmly is a tendency to generalize about her first contact with the class. If she does come to hasty conclusions, her own attitude may produce a vicious circle that only works to perpetuate a problem situation.

There are usually one or two children in a class who accept the teacher more quickly than the rest of the students. The teacher has to be careful about receiving their co-operation, however, because they typically are not the natural leaders of the group and frequently are either rejected by the other children or simply "different" from them. One of the big tasks in gaining rapport is to seek out the "natural" leaders and win their support. Two approaches can aid in this assignment. To the extent that the teacher demonstrates an understanding of the feelings of the deprived, the natural leaders, who typically reflect the cultural norms, will probably react favorably even though suspiciously at first. Then, too, if she does not accept uncritically the support of the children who are initially anxious to please her—the less typical members of the class—she is more likely to gain the respect of the real leaders and the class as a whole.

If the initial situation makes teaching difficult, if the children are unruly, the teacher should struggle to overcome this through an emphasis on learning; she should not cynically capitulate to the situation and attempt to run the class like a prison. The first step in this process would be to establish an unvarying routine with simple, clear, enforced rules. Classroom traditions should be built around the goal of learning. Step-by-step goals, signposts, and standards should be established.

The teacher should indicate that fighting is prohibited, not because it is wrong to defend oneself, but because it destroys the necessary classroom atmosphere conducive to learning.

The teacher should convey to the children that she understands why they have not done well in the past. She realizes that this is due in part to their moving about a good deal, to their not knowing the language and customs of the school, and she should make this known to the class. But now things are going to be different —their school difficulties can be overcome by hard work and a good understanding between them and herself.

The Auditory Set

The teacher should know that these children's auditory attention to adult speech has not been well rehearsed in their homes. These children are simply not used to listening to adults give "talks," and "parents and children seldom converse together except to exchange particular information or when parents give commands."[1] The parents do not attempt to entertain their children. Thus, when the children come to school they are not prepared to listen to the teacher talk for thirty or forty minutes at a stretch, and they are frequently bewildered. They do not know how to concentrate in this kind of situation, and their attention wanders. They are much more used to responding to their siblings and this response is quickly transferred to reacting to the other children in the class, rather than to the teacher. This, of course, easily leads to their becoming "behavior problems" and "poor learners."

The teacher will have to develop the auditory attention of these children; she will have to teach them how to listen, and constantly make sure that they understand what is being discussed. One interesting technique for achieving this goal was reported to us recently by a teacher who has had vast experience with deprived children. He said that when he asks a question in class like "What is six plus eight?" he tries to have every child answer the question regardless of whether the first child questioned gave the right answer. He goes around the room in this fashion so that

[1] Allison Davis, Burleigh B. Gardner, and Mary R. Gardner, *Deep South*, (Chicago: University of Chicago Press, 1941), pp. 102, 129.

no child can fall asleep. He makes a game out of it also; after all the answers are in, the class sees how many children got it right and how many got it wrong.[2]

This technique, of course, cannot be used indefinitely. It is too time consuming. But it is a good transitional technique for developing auditory attention in the classroom, and when this set has been developed, other approaches can come into play.

Developing Verbal Skills

While the deprived child has certain verbal difficulties, and tends to have a more physical pattern of communication, the teacher may enlist this physical style to develop verbal expression. In the early stages the disadvantaged child will express himself largely around things he can see and do. For example, after role-playing a situation, he can be remarkably verbal. He loves to talk about the scenes he has acted out or has seen other children act out. He finds this very exciting, and he is often keenly articulate in the discussion period that follows the role-playing action. This, of course, is one reason why the teacher can profitably employ role-playing as a stimulus for discussion. A problem arises, however, when the teacher comes to believe that deprived children can only articulate around things they can see and do. This can lead to an over-dependence on visual aids, role-playing, and the like. Actually, this may be necessary in the first stages— in the transition period in the school. But once the deprived child is awakened, through his visual and kinesthetic senses, he is able to progress to a more verbal, conceptual level, where verbalization can occur without immediate sensory cues. Thus in the role-playing example, the teacher will be able to arouse considerable discussion merely by reminding the children of the incident acted out on a previous day; she need not repeat the whole role-playing session in order to encourage verbal participation.

Of course, the process of developing the ability to verbalize is not nearly as simple as this; one role-playing session, one presentation of visual aids, is certainly not enough. Even after a primitive level of verbalization has been reached, periodic reinforcement by visual stimulation is necessary. This is true because verbalization and conceptualization are so intricately related to the senses in

[2] Personal communication from Winston Robbins, a teacher at the Henry Ittelson Center For Child Research in New York City.

the deprived individual. Verbalization may be *initiated* by sensory images, but it may also occur in its richest forms in the presence of non-verbal stimuli. The teacher must recognize that under-privileged children can verbalize independently of visual mate-rial, and that this ability increases as they become more involved in ideas. The process can be quickened to the extent that teachers verbally employ visual images as cues in introducing discussions.

Fear and Persistence

Deprived children have acquired a number of attitudes and fears that militate against learning. *Fear of failure* is significant in this regard. It is important that the teacher encourage the child, and indicate in every way possible that she expects the child to learn. Slow learning should not be penalized or looked down upon, and the teacher should be alert for slow, potentially gifted, children. Most important, deprived children do not respond well to being "challenged." They are too insecure and defensive. This is one of the reasons why they will rarely volunteer.

Despite their fears and general lack of school know-how, these children have educational potentialities that have rarely been utilized. While they are slow at getting involved in problems, once their interest is aroused, they seem to be able to work patiently and intensely for long hours at a stretch. They do not like to work in short spurts with frequent breaks. At first glance, this perseverance may seem at odds with the apathy they evi-dence in the school, and their fear of failure. Apparently it is only when they overcome their fears that perseverance and dogged problem-solving show themselves. If the teacher can bring them past their initial withdrawal and hostility, she may find person-ality characteristics that are valuable for learning. Not only will the persistence be in evidence, but the deprived child's maturity and feeling for functional responsibility may also come into play at this point. With the right approach, he may become a serious, disciplined student.

Teacher Selection

What kind of teacher is most effective with the disadvantaged child? The first answer that comes to mind is "one who likes to teach." Yet, this is too simple. Many teachers who like to teach, for many different reasons are not at home with these children. Some people like to teach because of the intellectual stimulation, and some because they are interested in children and their development. As one competent teacher put it, "There are teachers who want to teach *history* to children, and there are others who want to teach *children* history." It is the latter who do the most meaningful job with deprived children, or, for that matter, with any kind of handicapped child. The teachers who like the intellectual stimulation, the ones who come to "teach *history* to children," are likely to fare better with the more verbal, patently advanced child.[3]

Another factor that seems important is identification with the underdog. A teacher who possesses this feeling is more likely to understand the problems and feelings of the underprivileged youngster. No group has a monopoly on underdog identification. People who themselves come from a deprived background sometimes identify with this group and sometimes reject their origins, while many middle-class individuals have strong feelings for the "guy who is down." (Of course, there are other reasons for wanting teachers who come from an underprivileged background. Regardless of whether or not they reject their origins, they frequently have surprising "savvy" about the children and their ways, which can be useful.)

Sexton notes that the teacher with the reformer's zeal is most needed in deprived areas, but that often these individuals are unwelcome in the school.

> Unfortunately, reformers are often eccentric in their habits. They are not always well-mannered, well-dressed, and well-behaved, much less likable. They disagree, they argue, and they are active rather than passive in temperament. They want to change things. They are not always pleasant with their superiors. Often, with their colleagues, they are not 'one of the boys.'
>
> But, offensive as their behavior may sometimes be, such reformers are rather desperately needed. The schools, therefore, not only should make a place for them, but should actively seek them out and encourage them to teach, however troublesome they may prove to be.[4]

[3] Personal communication from Shelly Koenigsberg, former public school teacher in Baltimore, Maryland.

[4] Patricia Sexton, *Education and Income,* (New York: The Viking Press, Inc., 1961), p. 233.

Physical, somewhat less word-ridden, people make good teachers for disadvantaged children also. They appear to be able to communicate with these children on many levels and through varied media. The children accept them more readily as models after whom to pattern themselves.

Last and by no means least, it is the dedicated teacher who is most influential with the educationally handicapped child. The teacher who "came to teach"—not the one who has a "job in the school"—is far more effective. Unfortunately, the cynicism that pervades much of the school system, including the teacher training institutes, does not foster dedication. For a real breakthrough to take place, the contemptuous attitude held by many educators, as well as non-educators, toward the occupation of teacher must be battled out, so that we can begin to win more teachers who are proud to teach.

A STORY OF ONE TEACHER

Perhaps one of the best ways to discuss effective teaching is to report an interview with a teacher who has had marked success with deprived children. We talked with Miss L. at some length about how she handled the problems of "bad" language, discipline, fighting, rules, developing interest in remote subjects, relationships to parents.

Miss L. told us she starts her first class with a full question-and-answer discussion of what she calls the ground rules of the course. She begins:

"You and I are going to live together for the next year. To get along, what will we have to do? What problems will we face and how can we handle them?" In the course of this first meeting she states:

"I am here to teach; you are here to learn. I want you to tell what I can do to help you. Now, to do this we need some rules." She then asks them to discuss why certain rules, such as "no running in class," are necessary. During the hour some child will usually raise his hand and ask whether he can get a drink of water. In response she says, "You're too old to *ask* for water; *tell me* you want a drink, and unless I need you here that very minute it will be OK with me if you go."

Another thing that happens every opening day is the "initiation" of the teacher. "This is a highly organized, cooperative effort to break the new teacher. They want to see how smart you are, how much you can stand. So one child says it's too light in the room—can we pull down the shades. Then another one complains it's too dark—can we pull them up. Somebody else is too warm and wants the windows open, while still another party is too cold. This is a game the kids love to play."

And what is the teacher supposed to do, we asked? "Stand firm, show that you're wise to the game, kid about it, but don't go along with it. You are the master of the ship and you will decide when it's too cold, too light, and so on. Always remember the class is your fortress."

After about three weeks the class has a period of mutual evaluation in which they discuss how well the teacher has been living up to her part of the bargain, and vice versa. Some child may tell her that she hasn't paid enough attention to some other child. When the criticisms are accurate, "and they often are," she accepts them and attempts to correct the situation. The children learn soon that they can depend on her, that she will stand by what she says. For example, one day the teacher stated that a news story appearing in the *New York Daily News* was also in *The New York Times*. The children said it wasn't. Miss L. replied that she would eat the newspaper if it wasn't in the *Times*, because she was so dead sure she was right. The following day she discovered that she had been wrong, whereupon she obtained a cake from the school cafeteria, stuffed the newspaper inside of it, and ate it in front of the entire class. This is what sociologists like to call the "propaganda of the deed." Interestingly enough, the children knew in advance that she would live up to her word, and some of them expressed apprehension at showing her the newspaper because they were afraid she would get sick when she ate it.

We asked Miss L. what she did when the rules were disobeyed. "I never have them clean the board or anything like that as punishment. We all share in cleaning up and it isn't a punishment. Nor do I give them a learning assignment to do because a punishment should simply be a waste of time, and should not be confused with learning. What I do is merely give them a great many foolish sentences to write, read them carefully to check that they have done them correctly, and then tear them up and throw them away. I want them to realize that the task is just a waste of time. If the situation is very serious, I call up the parents and explain to them in front of the child that he is not letting me teach him. But I don't call the parents just when something goes wrong. I try to call them every time the child does something especially delightful, and so I have basic contact with them. I don't want my relationship to parents simply geared to discipline, so that every time they hear my voice, they automatically say to themselves, 'What has Billy done this time?' If they hear from me about the positive, exciting things that Billy does, their reaction to the misbehavior will take place in a much better mood.

"Another thing about discipline—when I apply the rules, I never get indignant and I don't humiliate the child. The rules are purely objective and I'm only 'sorry' that they have violated them and therefore require punishment. I get the children to realize that all of us have to accept the consequences of our behavior. And I repeat over and over again that breaking the rules means 'I can't teach you, I can only think you do not want to learn.' Of course, punishment and threats should be rare— you shouldn't have to punish children often. It's more of a last resort and loses its meaning if it becomes habitual. For most common occurrences, I am more prone to say to the disobeying child, 'You are letting me down—you're breaking our agreement.' One thing is certain, these kids want limits. It's time we got over the idea that discipline means rigidity and dictatorship. The deprived child thrives on rules and order, and if he respects and likes you, he hasn't the least desire to rebel. He wants you to be firm, but responsive. Firmness doesn't mean brutality or hardness. To brutality he responds in kind, and then the classroom becomes a jungle.

"Firmness has got to be tied to clearly designated rules and requirements. For example, one day an education major, who was working as an assistant group leader with a group of children, organized a little party with her group. The children cooked spaghetti and had a feast. When they finished, they started to run around and play. She became angry because they weren't willing to wash the dishes and she started to threaten them with all sorts of disciplinary actions. As far as she was concerned, they were being most disobedient. But she hadn't told them from the very beginning what they were expected to do. She didn't tell them that the party consisted of cooking the food, eating it, and then doing the dishes. Instead, she took it for granted, but they didn't and so they felt as though the dish-washing had been sprung on them from out of nowhere. She hadn't organized the whole thing with a clear designation of tasks, so in a sense they really hadn't disobeyed. Of course, at a later stage, when you have built up a tradition of authority with the children, you can spring a new rule at the last minute and they will obey you. Even then this is not a terribly good idea, and it is completely impractical for a new teacher, or a teacher in a transitory situation, where her authority has not had sufficient time to be fully accepted. Authority and discipline go hand in hand. And authority has to be developed day by day, through clear statements and application of rules and regulations, and lots of repetition."

What do you do, we asked, when a child gets angry at you and actually rebels?

"Oh, a child will sometimes say 'Who do you think you are?' I answer with all the dignity I can muster, 'I am *your teacher.*' And if a child threatens to hit me, I say, 'I don't think you'd do a thing like that—I am your teacher.' Usually, if the children are behaving this way, they need more exercise. I find that a very good practice is to have the children take fairly frequent breaks during which they do calisthenics and deep breathing. This lets off a lot of steam, gives them some fresh air, and relaxes them. Breaks are also particularly good because, in the early transition to the school, they are not used to paying attention for long periods of time."

We then queried Miss L. on what she did when the children used vile language.

"Mainly roll with the punches, never get flabbergasted, show that you know the lingo, and are not 'stuck up.' Answer or deal with whatever they have said irrespective of the language, and then, as sort of an afterthought, remark that 'we do not use that kind of language in this class, please.' And don't think I haven't gotten unrequested apologies, sometimes as much as a week later."

How about fighting—what do you do about that, we asked? "I make it perfectly clear that I have nothing against fighting, that it's OK to know how to defend yourself, but in my classroom I can't teach you if there are going to be fisticuffs. If a fight is already in progress, I very often ask the two or three biggest boys in the class to help break it up—if they are not already involved in it, that is. Or sometimes I tap one of the combatants on the shoulder and ask if he has a match."

Turning to the problem of learning, we asked Miss L. what she did about motivating the children to learn.

"One day, as I came into a class in which I was a sub, I overheard a couple of Negro children arguing about who was darker and why. I said 'Do you want to talk about that; are you interested?' Then I went into a long discussion of physical anthropology, genetics, and race. The children sat enrapt and wouldn't let me erase the words from the board until they had carefully copied them down!"

But, Miss L. added, this kind of example can be misleading because "teaching these children requires the utmost planning. You cannot play it by ear. You must know which questions you are going to ask each level of student in the class. You have to think through how you can involve each one. At the same time, you can't plan more than one or two lessons in advance. Every inch of progress on the part of the child is something that calls for genuine praise. Even trying, staying with something, must be fully appreciated—as it is a sign of maturity—an important step forward."

What about the basic structure of the lesson plan—how is this dealt with, we wondered?

"Well, for one thing, the typical demonstration lesson given in most schools won't work. The teacher can't get up and demonstrate long division, ask for questions, and then assume the children have understood it and will be able to do the homework. Initially, at least, there will be too many children in the class who don't have the requisite knowledge for learning long division. Some don't know how to add and subtract, others don't know how to read. And practically none of them are used to learning from a simple lecture demonstration. They have to be worked with individually and in small groups. And they have to do the problems in front of you—not just hear how they are done. As often as not, they won't know what questions to ask just from hearing a lecture. Homework cannot be counted on—in the early stages anyway—and so the work must be carried on in the classroom."

The Three Stages: Rapport, Fascination, and Power

Our next question concerned the problem of motivating these children to learn, and enlisting their interest in subjects that are not directly tied to their lives. Miss L. said that she didn't accept the widely held notion that disadvantaged children could *only* be interested in topics by showing them a direct relationship between the topic and their own lives.

"In the first stage of your relationship to the class, this may be true. But once you have established a basic relationship to them, you can teach them anything. This is what I call the second stage. Here your own excitement, your fascination with the topic, spreads to the children, who at this stage identify with you so much that your enthusiasm is contagious. I remember once saying to a class that I hadn't been interested in baseball, but if so many people were fascinated by it, there must be something to it and I wanted to find out what it was. Then I suggested to them that there were a great many things which they didn't know about that fascinated me and lots of other people, and perhaps they would find these subjects equally wonderful if they gave them a chance."

We asked Miss L. whether there were any further stages in her scheme. She responded, "Yes, there is a third and last stage that you aim for, but in which you only succeed with some children. The first stage is where you motivate the child in terms of his own interests and build a mutual acceptance. At the second stage his liking for you, and perhaps strong identification with you, allows him to consider topics that have no intrinsic interest for him in terms of his immediate experience. Here you have *won him to learning* for its own sake; you have lit the flame. The third stage is where the child begins to feel his own power, begins to realize what *he* can do with knowledge, sees the value of his own ideas, no matter how primitive. This child can now play a role in helping other, less-developed children. The seeds of creativity have been planted. This happens with a few children every year and it's what gives teaching a real kick when it does. This child doesn't need a good teacher anymore. He can move to a new neighborhood, have his school life disrupted, and still come back strong. The desire for learning is in him now along with some confidence. This is the stage of power."

The Development of a Good Teacher

The development of good teachers is not nearly so difficult a task as it has sometimes been painted. Even if we follow the age-old dictum that "great teachers are born and not made" (and while this may have validity with regard to *great* teachers, it is not equally true of *good* teachers)—there is still an awful lot of good teaching potential in people that needs to be nurtured. A teacher may have lots of potential, but not know how to use it, and in particular not know what is required in teaching disadvantaged children in a setting in which the school and the child have been separated for some time. In other words, teaching educationally deprived children in a healthy school environment is one thing, but teaching them in a mutually embittered atmosphere is quite another matter, and the new teacher cannot be given any rosy pictures of this assignment. At the same time, she can come to realize and see for herself that if she gets past the first stage of achieving classroom rapport and enlisting interest (most teachers do not effectively achieve this stage with deprived children, and those who do rarely go beyond it to the second stage of learning), then she may have an exciting time with the class. She has to overcome the cultural barrier at Stage One—this is the big task—and then there may be smooth sailing.

In order to do this she not only has to be prepared in terms of all the things we have talked about in connection with teaching these children—a solid knowledge of their culture, techniques for gaining classroom rapport, and so on—but she must see effective teachers doing the job. She should see teachers tackle the Stage One problem of winning the class, establishing a routine and her own authority; and she should also see teachers working with a class at Stage Two, where they have been "won to learning." Both are important, because if she hasn't seen Stage Two, she will not believe it possible to have this kind of positive experience with disadvantaged children. And if she *only* sees Stage Two, she will not be honestly prepared for the real problems of Stage One. At present in New York City, Higher Horizons teachers have been going from school to school demonstrating classroom approaches, particularly the tasks involved in gaining control of the teacher's fortress, the classroom.

Still, the new teacher cannot easily emulate the pattern and style of the experienced teacher. She feels differently "inside," and she does not yet possess a repertoire of fluid approaches that have developed out of her own experience. One of the best ways to meet this problem is through the use of role-playing in the teacher training programs. Situations can be set up so that the new teacher can act out the approaches she has been hearing about and seeing. Her fellow students in training can "play" the class. Roles can then be reversed so that each individual learns what it feels like to be a teacher and an underprivileged pupil. Each can come to see how the teacher looks to these children. The discussion can point out what the teacher did that was wrong and how it could be improved. Then, in the permissive practice atmosphere of the role-playing, setting new methods based on the suggestions of the group can be tried out. Someone in the group can take the new teacher's role, thus showing her how she looks as a teacher. This provides her with a valuable mirror, which is far better than just a discussion of errors, and it furnishes the basis for a much more pointed and meaningful discussion.

One of the special values of role-playing sessions is that the new teacher, or the student teacher, can discover and develop her own repertoire of skills. For example, we often suggest that a teacher in a deprived setting express herself physically and visually as much as possible: walk around the room, use gestures, touch the children, etc. But for many people this is simply not possible; it is not within the framework of their personality, and there is nothing more dangerous than attempting to manufacture a style for which you have no feeling. It will go over like a lead balloon. The teacher will feel stiff and uneasy in imitating what "doesn't come naturally," and the children, who are surprisingly sensitive, will know it is contrived. The role-playing sessions will soon ascertain whether the new teacher has any potential feeling for this "physical" pattern. If the teacher does, the ensuing sessions can bring out this potential, can encourage her, and can help her to shape her future style. If she does not have this particular skill, no matter, because fortunately there are innumerable ways of being an effective teacher, and role-playing can assist in finding and integrating the best approaches for the particular teacher. Depending on what kind of personality style she has, she will probably select different approaches and techniques from the things we have suggested. If she is a careful, meticulous person herself, she can perhaps synchronize more readily with the slow style of the disadvantaged child. If she has great patience, she may be able to appreciate the tenacious persistence that evidences itself in these children once they become absorbed, and she may be able to bring them to this point more rapidly. If she is vivid and exciting, and much interested in the subject, she should be encouraged to impart this enthusiasm to the children. If the teacher is a physically strong man, he should convey this to the children, not by display of his prowess, but by what one counselor at Wiltwick so aptly called the "suggestion of strength" —"you never hit the kid, but your size and strength are always *there,* by the way you touch the boy, lift things, handle yourself, and so on."

But strength, of course, is not only established through the physical. The thin, small-voiced female teacher can be just as effective as the big baritone. Role-playing should help the new teacher to discover the manifold sources of strength and authority, and particularly her own resources in this capacity. Strength can be reflected to these children by definiteness, quiet, firm tones, consistency, standing by a statement, determination to teach, and so on. It is a tremendous mistake to think that authority and respect can only be commanded through physical power. The climax in role-playing comes when the new teacher begins to feel and act in the sessions as though the classroom were her fortress. You cannot tell people to be confident— but you can provide the conditions, knowledge, and practice that build confidence. Role-playing is one of the best confidence builders we know of for the new teacher.

xi

HIGHER HORIZONS:

A CRITICAL EVALUATION

It is practically impossible to pick up a popular article related to education these days without reading about the program known as Higher Horizons, initially called The Demonstration Guidance Project. This project, begun in 1956 at Junior High School No. 43 in New York City, has literally swept the country as a model to be emulated. Similar projects have arisen in thirteen major cities (The Great Cities Improvement Project), including Baltimore, Buffalo, Boston, Chicago, Cleveland, Detroit, Los Angeles, Milwaukee, Philadelphia, Pittsburgh, San Francisco, St. Louis, and Washington. No program for the "culturally deprived" child has ever enjoyed such publicity. Despite basic weaknesses, to which we will turn later, this project has demonstrated convincingly that supposedly uneducable children from lower socio-economic backgrounds can successfully learn and progress in a reorganized school environment.

The original aim of the Higher Horizons experiment was "to identify, stimulate, and guide into college channels able students from low socio-economic homes."[1] It was part of a large group of Operation Talent Search ventures that have sprung up all over the country during the last five years. The Project was later broadened to include all levels of students. This new program is

[1] The quotations cited on the following pages are taken from *Strengthening Democracy*, Vol. 9, No. 4, March–April, 1957, and Vol. 12, No. 4, May, 1960, published by the Board of Education of the City of New York.

now in effect in thirteen junior high schools and thirty-one elementary schools in New York City, serving about 12,500 pupils.[2]

The philosophy embodied in Higher Horizons is best seen in the following quotation:

> Many children from families of low socio-economic status do not reach their maximum achievement level in the ordinary school program. Handicapped by culturally impoverished homes that lack an educational tradition, they often record scores on tests of mental ability that do not reveal their full intellectual potential. Nor do such children usually match the academic achievement demonstrated by their more privileged fellow pupils of comparable ability.
>
> The needs of children living in culturally and economically depressed areas are especially acute since, for most of them, school is their only positive experience in life.

Propaganda of the Deed

The success of the Demonstration Guidance Project has been outstanding: reading ability and grades improved, I.Q.'s went up, school attendance increased, discipline problems subsided, and parents' participation in the school rose.

The academic record of the Project group that entered George Washington High School has shown great improvement over that of pre-project students. In 1953, 5 out of 105 students passed all their courses at the end of the first year, while in 1958, 43 out of 111 passed all their subjects. Previously, only two boys had averages better than 80 per cent, while in the 1958 Project group sixteen did. In 1960, 39 per cent more students graduated from George Washington High School than did before the Project was begun, and three and one-half times as many went on to college. More than half showed definite gains in I.Q. scores, with some increases up to 40 points.

Attendance figures at Junior High School No. 43 indicate that there are an average of 30 additional pupils in school every day, compared to pre-project figures.

Throughout New York City only 10 per cent of Junior high school parents attend daytime meetings but 23 per cent of 43's

[2] The success of the Program reported on the following pages refers, in the main, to the original Demonstration Guidance Project; the effectiveness of the expanded Program is now in the process of being evaluated.

parents met throughout the year to learn how they could contribute to the project's success.

During the first year of the Program there were over 800 contacts with parents, and many volunteered to take small groups of children on trips on Saturdays and Sundays.

How Did They Do It?

The Program stressed a number of outstanding features:

1. A variety of instruments were utilized, including a nonverbal I.Q. test, in order to assess the ability of the students— "It is possible that each instrument may reveal abilities which another instrument may overlook."

2. Pictures of Negro and Puerto Rican doctors, nuclear physicists, and journalists were displayed in the classrooms to instill motivation and improve the children's "self-image."

3. Special remedial reading classes of five and six pupils each were organized to improve the basic reading deficit. All the teachers, regardless of what subjects they taught, devoted the first ten minutes of each class to drills in reading.

4. Book fairs and circulating libraries of paperbacks were started in the schools to stimulate reading. Children who read a certain number of books were given buttons and badges: "Readers are Leaders."

5. An intensive counseling service was established to provide guidance concerning college and career possibilities.

6. An intensive cultural program was initiated to acquaint the children with "good music," etc., and to broaden their tastes. Children were not simply subjected to concerts, plays, and other cultural events, but were rather more carefully prepared for them in advance.

7. Classrooms were opened after school hours giving children, who came from crowded, noisy homes, the opportunity for quiet study.

In order to provide some flavor of the approach employed, let us present two of the features in the Program's own words.

Parent Involvement

   Daytime meetings were held with parents on all grade levels to acquaint them with the aims of the Demonstration Guidance

Project and to gain their cooperation. Official class teachers were relieved of class assignments to enable them to be present. An evening meeting was arranged for those parents who could not attend during the day.

Where parents could not come to a day or evening meeting, plans were made for visits to the home by the social case worker. To keep parents informed and to gain their active support, letters were sent home explaining trips and other special features. Workshops were organized to give parents the opportunity to discuss career possibilities for their children.

If parents could not meet counselors during working hours, the appointments would be scheduled early in the morning or at night. One counselor had meetings with parents on 14 successive Sundays.

Counselors made arrangements with parents in crowded apartments to turn television sets off between certain hours so students could complete homework and hammered out agreements with younger brothers and sisters to permit budding scholars to work without interruption.

"Raising Cultural Sights"

To encourage the enjoyment of good music, the school purchased sixty subscriptions to the Young People's Philharmonic-Symphony Orchestra series of five concerts. About 300 pupils benefitted from the experience of going to Carnegie Hall for the Saturday concerts. As preparation, children learned the composition of the symphony orchestra and compared it with other types of orchestras with which they might be more familiar. They discussed the composers whose works they were to hear, their lives and their times. They were given a list of things to look for and they listened to the compositions to be played at the concert.

After the first concert, pupils who attented recorded their reactions in a group discussion of the event. This revealed that, despite the initial reluctance of some to go, all enjoyed the experience and many asked to go again. As a result, it was decided to allow one third of those attending the next concert to be repeaters.

Many obstacles had to be overcome in stimulating pupil attendance at the first concert. Pupils had had no concert experience and so were unwilling to go. Many children felt they could get all the music they wanted from recordings. Some parents were reluctant to permit children to travel downtown. Others objected to their children's losing time and money gained from out-of-school jobs or to losing their children's assistance at home. Personal interviews were used to convince pupils and parents of the values of the experience. Teachers generated enthusiasm for the trip.

Fifty-five students and five teachers attended the concert. The fifty cent admission and the carfare of those who could not afford the outlay were paid by the school project scholarship fund.

Some of the children wished that their parents could come, so some parents were invited to future concerts and a sitter provided where necessary. If a pupil who could not afford to lose a day's pay wanted to go, the scholarship fund was tapped to reimburse him.

The school purchased tickets for performances of Shakespeare's *Taming of the Shrew* and the Metropolitan Opera production of *Tosca*.

Three seventh-year social studies classes that were studying New York State gained first-hand knowledge of the Hudson River Valley on a bus journey to the Hyde Park home of Franklin D. Roosevelt. For many of the children, this visit to an historic site was their first such experience outside of New York City.

Other activities included in the Program were: visits to the Museum of Modern Art and the Metropolitan Museum of Art; trips to Bellevue Hospital, Brookhaven Laboratories, West Point, and the Ford Motor Company; attendance at movies and plays including *War and Peace, Moby Dick, Inherit the Wind, Take a Giant Step,* Shaw's *Man of Destiny, The Diary of Ann Frank.*

Hope in an Age of Non-Belief

It would be easy simply to report the apparent success of the Program and let it go at that. But while, perhaps, inspirational, this would not be entirely accurate. Before turning to the major criticisms that must be made, some words are in order about its contributions.

Most outstanding is the smashing defeat rendered the environmental determinism of our times, which so pessimistically assumes that a difficult early environment cannot be counteracted or overcome. The Program demonstrates enormous belief in an era paralyzed by cynicism and defeatism. It has belief that the non-favored children can learn, and so they do. It has faith that the parents will help the teachers, and they do. It has hope that tired, fear-ridden teachers can become devoted and energetic, and they do. These alone are earth-shaking contributions in an age of "blandocracy," marked by the "end of ideology."

Despite its hopefulness the Program has been marked by realistic, hard-headed, down-to-earthness. Its faith has not clouded its vision. Rose-colored glasses, pollyanna phrases, and exaggerated claims have not been part of its repertoire.

Education or Placebo?

At a cursory glance our first major criticism may appear strictly methodological, but on closer inspection its substantive nature will become clearer.

There is no question that the Program did a splendid job in demonstrating conclusively that educationally deprived children can learn. The point at issue is whether the Program itself produced this learning. Is it possible that the achievements did not come about from the announced methods of the Project, but are a by-product of the experiment itself? What does this mean? In order to consider this possibility it will be necessary to go back to a now-famous social science investigation.

Some years ago a classic experiment took place at Western Electric that discovered something which has come to be known as the "Hawthorn Effect."[3] Here, factory workers' production and morale were greatly enhanced by putting them in special groups and varying the lighting in the rooms. At first, the results seemed obvious, because with better lighting, production went up. But then it was discovered that similar increases in production occurred when the lighting was decreased! Apparently, the very setting up of special experimental groups, and the concomitant attention, was sufficient to produce the observed results. This kind of placebo effect is similar to that found in modern medicine, where people appear to be cured by some drug, while actually the simple taking of a pill containing no drug is often sufficient to produce the same effect.

[3] See F. J. Roethligsberger and W. J. Dickson, *Management and the Worker* (Cambridge: Harvard University Press, 1939).

One can only wonder whether a similar process is at work in the Higher Horizons success story. After all, a great deal of excitement was engendered by the newness of the experiment, the positive democratic goals, the increased input of effort and resources. Any one, or all, of these factors may have stimulated enough enthusiasm to achieve the obtained results, independent of the specific methodology employed. In addition, another variable may have been operative in this situation. Deprived children have been notoriously neglected by the school system, and perhaps the very fact of their neglect has been the decisive one in their hitherto poor performances. Higher Horizons came along, and quite apart from its specific approaches, the underprivileged children were given a great deal of attention. Conceivably, this may have been enough to produce the findings.

Regardless of the possibility of the placebo effect, the very nature of this experiment makes it difficult to ascertain which variables produced the results. Was it the smaller classes, the carefully picked teachers, the special efforts to involve the parents, the free trips to concerts, or any other of a dozen different factors, that led to the improvement in work and morale?

It might be objected, "Who cares which variables were decisive; the important thing is they got the results." Unfortunately, the naive pragmatism underlying this defense is not even good pragmatism. *We need to develop approaches that will be effective on a large scale in the everyday school setting*, where teachers are not working day and night and 14 Sundays per term! We need techniques that can be applied by the average teacher, hopefully with a fair amount of devotion, but not necessarily the short-lived zeal fostered by a unique experiment. There are an increasing number of reports that as the Project has spread, the enthusiasm of the overworked teachers has begun to wane.

The Project is a special demonstration program where enormous resources, money, and energy are poured into a relatively small area.

> On the average, a junior high school educational and vocational counselor in New York City has a pupil load of about 2000. In this project it was fewer than 400.
> The Project also featured an expanded group guidance program using increased library materials and audio-visual aids, in-

spirational assembly programs, and community resources. The plan included a limited number of $5 weekly grants-in-aid to enable pupils who would otherwise have to seek after-school jobs to meet their financial needs. The first-year budget for the program, covering 1600 junior high school pupils, was originally estimated at $44,000. It was supplemented by funds added by the Board of Education for three remedial teaching positions.

The Program is intended as a showpiece, a demonstration. In a sense it is constructive propaganda. An effort is made to convince the world that it can be done, and clearly it can. This is a worthy demonstration. But what is illustrated by this concentrated effort may not be as easily applicable in the everyday school setting, short of a major reorganization of the educational system. Moreover, any such special program engenders enthusiasm that might not carry over into the normal setting. For these reasons it is particularly necessary to try to determine what features of the Program may be decisively effective. Furthermore, we need to know which aspects are transferable to other, non-experimental, schools where special resources may be less available.

These criticisms do not in any way deny what might be called the "face validity" of the techniques employed. We do not doubt for a moment that more tutoring, increased emphasis on reading, a larger number of teachers, and so on, are valuable in and of themselves. The Program makes it difficult to assess which of the manifold changes are decisive, and which combinations of changes get the most mileage.

To some degree, the methodological difficulties we have cited are insurmountable in any action research program, but the flair for visible success heightens these problems in demonstration focused projects like Higher Horizons.

The Ideology of Deprivation

Despite the hopefulness of the experiment, there is a pronounced tendency to underestimate the underprivileged. There is the seeming implication that the disadvantaged had pretty much surrendered to their environment until the school came along to help them.

This view is highlighted in the quotation cited previously:

"The needs of children living in culturally and economically depressed areas are especially acute since, for most of them, *school is their only positive experience in life*." (Our emphasis.) This viewpoint overlooks the many cooperative characteristics of family life and child rearing, the enjoyment of music, humor, the down-to-earth, informal, human relationships. It overlooks the angry protest that has begun to reap rewards in the South as well as gain national recognition. We cannot believe that school is the only worthwhile experience of these groups. Perhaps even more disturbing is the fact that the Higher Horizons approach requires us to believe that whatever change appears in the deprived comes entirely from the *outside*. Aside from the ethnocentricity and inaccuracy of this view, it leads to considerable difficulty at the action level. We believe that it is much easier to work with people and even to change them in certain directions—such as expanding their artistic interests—when the sources of the change are seen to exist within the people themselves. If, in fact, education were the only positive thing in the life of the underprivileged person, then the task would be herculean indeed. On the other hand, if positive traits already exist that can be built upon, the job is much more feasible, and rapport easier to establish. Underestimation of the deprived child makes the educator's work that much more difficult. Thus, even if there be any doubt about our position concerning positive characteristics of lower socio-economic groups—unless there is certainty that there is no shred of truth in this view—it might prove wise to adopt it as a working hypothesis, a positive myth, because by so doing we can work *with* the underprivileged rather than *upon* them.

No Self-Blame

Another characteristic of the Program that indirectly contributes to the accent on the limitations of the underprivileged is the failure to place any explicit blame on the school or the teacher for the existing separation between school and child. There is practically no genuine self-criticism concerning the attitudes of the school toward the deprived child. The underlying view seems rather to be that the difficulties experienced by the child in the school system stem primarily from *his* inadequacies—the "lack of an educational tradition," "inadequate motivation," the need to leave school for a job, and the like. These things are, of course, true, but the school, too, contributes to the problem by undervaluing the culture of the deprived, by employing teachers who dislike teaching these children, by using readers whose themes and symbols are foreign to the children, and so on. The school has to face its share of responsibility in having produced the schism that prevails, and must not simply emphasize the background limitations of the disadvantaged.

The Higher Horizons Program shows little awareness that the discrimination practiced in the school has produced justifiable anger and alienation in these children and their parents. The protest and anger that is so admired when it takes place in the South, is poorly perceived and badly misunderstood when it occurs in our Northern schools. Frequently, the antagonism toward education that is blithely attributed to the underprivileged should be more accurately understood as a dislike for the school rather than education.

"Good Culture" or More Culture?

We should like also to note a number of relatively minor criticisms that further highlight the weaknesses of the experiment.

The educational program of Higher Horizons, while excellent in most respects, seems weighted on the artistic-literary side, with a consequent lack of emphasis on the social and physical sciences. Moreover, with regard to the cultural program itself, the aim of which is to have the children "learn to enjoy *good* music," (our emphasis) etc., we do not always know the rationale for the selection of the various activities. There are a number of superb choices, to be sure, like the trip to Hyde Park, the plays *Take a Giant Step* and *Inherit the Wind*. A visit to Hyde Park is a fine choice in light of the popularity of Franklin Roosevelt among the underprivileged. Pictures of F.D.R. still hang in many of their homes, and Negro children are frequently named Roosevelt Brown, Roosevelt Jones, etc. But we cannot be sure whether the trip was planned with these things in mind or to give social studies students who "were studying New York State" the opportunity of "gaining first-hand knowledge of the Hudson River Valley." And we wonder a bit at the selection of Shaw's *Man of Destiny*, as well as *Tosca, Taming of the Shrew, War and Peace*, and the visit to the Museum of Modern Art, all of which are activities unlikely to draw upon latent interests in the deprived child. The theme and background of *War and Peace* are not readily assimilated into the traditions of the deprived child.

Moreover, even when a particularly excellent selection is made, such as the play *Inherit the Wind*, one cannot be entirely sure, in light of some of the other selections, that its full potential value is explicitly recognized or anticipated. It is an exceptional play for underprivileged children because of the counterposition of two of their cardinal values: old time religion and modern science, to say nothing of their underdog identification, which surely should be enlisted by this story. The point we are making is not that any particular play be selected, but choices should not simply be dictated by a desire to impart "high culture"; they should be consciously planned in terms of how congruent they might be with the existing culture and values of the children concerned. We are not suggesting that these children cannot ultimately become interested in plays by Shaw or books by Tolstoy, but rather that cultural activities which have some relationship to their backgrounds would be far more appealing and could therefore lead more rapidly to the development of wider artistic appreciation. Initially, at least, there has to be a period of transition, in which artistic activities are very carefully selected in terms of the existing cultural interests of the underprivileged groups. It is most striking that the Program does not appear to stress Negro music or any of the ethnic contributions which these children are likely to have experienced. Probably one of the best ways of broadening cultural development—and we say "broadening" advisedly, rather than "beginning"—would be to use the existing cultural contributions of the various ethnic groups involved, and then to try to relate these interests to other, wider, cultural pursuits.

A Different Mental Style

Although the limitations of the standard tests are recognized in the Program, nevertheless in attempting to identify able students, a non-verbal intelligence test was utilized, along with a number of other achievement tests.

The Program does not appear to realize that the deprived child's difficulty with tests is not simply verbal inadequacy or lack of familiarity with standard words. This is one factor, but equally important are his lack of basic test-taking skills, insufficient practice, little motivation, and absence of rapport with the middle-class examiner. Haggard demonstrated that when these things were corrected the child improved enormously on the standard tests, despite the cultural bias of these instruments.

In attempting to identify able deprived students, there is little if any recognition that while the style of these children is far more slow, this may have its unique advantages. The concept of the *slow gifted child* is not considered by the Program, and one has the feeling that the able children who are selected probably resemble more the traditional, fast symbolic learners. The possibility of discovering a new kind of talent characterized by different ways of learning and thinking is bypassed by the Program, which appears to have a middle-class model in mind; the aim is to give the deprived children the experiences the more favored children have had, in the hope they might then develop along the lines of these children. Rarely considered is a genuine pluralism, where children of diverse backgrounds would be encouraged to develop very differently in light of their specific strengths and particular learning styles.

The "Demonstration" Ideology

What are the underlying ideological roots of the Higher Horizons movement? Why is there so much concern with detecting potential talent under every stone in America today? There appear to be at least three reasons:

1. The economic and scientific competition with the Soviet world:

> As long as the problem of the culturally deprived remains unsolved, potentially great scientists, mathematicians, social scientists, linguists, and others with talent will remain undiscovered and the *waste of human resources will continue.*[4]

2. The desire to prove to the as-yet-neutral portions of the globe that we are fundamentally democratic, and that the disadvantaged are not ignored in the affluent society:

[4] The Great Cities Improvement Studies Project, Ford Foundation Project, mimeographed, 1960.

The growing problem of the culturally deprived child as it is seen by travelers in the streets of the great cities of America, read about in newspapers, periodicals, and books, and viewed on cinema and television screens everywhere is distorting the *world concept of the American image*. This cannot help but degrade *American world leadership* and hinder the spreading of respect for the worth and dignity of the individual.[5]

3. The rise in juvenile delinquency, especially the appearance of the violent gang with its latent threat to middle-class mores, and the expenses incurred in its control:

> *The fiscal resources* of the nation will continue to be drained unnecessarily, severely, and increasingly, by the necessity for growing appropriations of public money for special services for education, welfare, and crime control.[6]

These three factors subtly shape and blend the new wave of educational concern for the deprived. Thus, there is more accent on discovering talent and on a college aimed program, rather than on a general education for all. So, too, most of the emphasis is on "demonstrations" where enormous resources are concentrated in small areas to insure a visible, democratic success for all the world to see. Finally, it is perhaps hoped that the underprivileged may be won to a middle-class way of life via education, and thus *violent* delinquency, at least, may subside. "Understanding and acceptance of the values and responsibilities of the prevailing urban culture" is one of the goals listed by the Great Cities Improvement Project.

Some of the reasons for the new wave of concern for the underprivileged may indeed be worthy. But none of them is *directly* concerned with the lower socio-economic groups themselves, and their aims and aspirations. This fact is closely connected with the faint patronization that we see in the Program, despite its very laudable intentions. A key point here is the fact that the Program is not noticeably informed about, or affected by, labor and minority group traditions.

Within the framework of these traditions, there are other reasons why such a program may be valuable, and, with certain modi-

5 *Ibid.*
6 *Ibid.*

fications, might win support from large groups of the under-privileged, including labor organizations, as well as from the genuinely liberal middle-class forces in the society. The spread of education is not only important in order to discover talent. Our own research investigations, as well as the findings of Arthur Kornhauser and Arnold Rose, indicate fairly clearly that increasing education does not necessarily "middle-classize" its recipients. Workers with more education were found to be more pro-union, to participate more in trade union activities, and to desire expanding labor organization. The more educated worker also indicated a greater acceptance of the political role of labor.[7] Thus, it is possible that the aid of the labor movement, which has hitherto not been greatly involved in the Higher Horizons type programs, might be enlisted. Moreover, from a general liberal point of view, expanding education is essential to democracy in order to combat anti-intellectualism.

To sum up:

The Higher Horizons Program represents a giant step forward, but it does not go far enough. Fundamentally, it symbolizes a curious amalgam of hope and underestimation. The perspective of the Program is essentially limited to that of the educator and his horizons. It considers the problems and conditions of the deprived person's life, but it does not stress the culture, the coping mechanisms, the "positives" of the underprivileged. Nor does it consider their understandable anger and resentment. On the other hand, the Program does demonstrate that the culturally deprived can be educated, and this is an extremely important service in the age of non-belief.

[7] See Frank Riessman, *Workers' Attitudes Toward Participation and Leadership*, unpublished Ph.D. dissertation, Columbia University, 1955.

xii

IDEAS FOR ACTION

This chapter provides a summary of the main arguments of the book by highlighting the policy recommendations implicit in our approach. While the action suggestions are largely directed toward educators, they have considerable bearing for psychiatrists and social workers, particularly those concerned with juvenile delinquents.

The Cultural Yardstick

Understand the culture of the underprivileged, including the positives. *This is not the same thing as recognizing the economic difficulties and general life conditions of the educationally deprived.* Most informed people are cognizant of the "deprived" side of the picture.

It is natural enough for educators to stress the liabilities, the deficiencies, of the underprivileged. These are the things that the teacher is confronted with all the time. The deprived child clearly is not happy at school, does not read well, appears unmotivated, is antagonistic to the teacher, possesses no well-formulated career plans, has no quiet place to study. These are the things that are easiest to see because they are on the surface. To see his strengths, and positive struggles, requires a deeper, more penetrating look.

Many people see only the negative environmental conditions

that surround the disadvantaged, and they believe that this *is* the culture. They feel that it is democratic and liberal to "accept" this culture (as just another way of life). But understanding of this culture must include a genuine appreciation of the positives that have arisen out of the effort, however insufficient at times, to cope with the difficult environment.

This is different from the standard view, which, by accenting deprivation, emphasizes weakness. In fact, one of the great difficulties with formulations like "culturally deprived," "disadvantaged," "culturally handicapped," "impoverished," and the like, is that they connote inadequacy, rather than present a rounded picture of the culture which would have to include strengths as well as deficiencies. We feel that our view is not only a fuller, more accurate, portrayal, but that it also constrains against snobbery and patronization. Weakness seen in the context of strength has a different meaning. It is difficult to patronize someone whose strengths you are well aware. To the extent that genuine cultural understanding takes place, there will be improvement in the problems of rapport in the classroom, the guidance office, and the Parent-Teacher Association.

If possible, teachers and psychologists should try to become interested in the nature and substance of the culture of disadvantaged groups and to find elements in it that they like, rather than endeavoring to understand it merely for practical purposes.

I.Q. Implications

At present the standard intelligence tests, both individual and group, are strongly middle-class biased. Educators should be cautious about using these tests on, or making inferences from them about, educationally deprived children. Placement of these children in special classes (retarded classes, adjustment classes) on the basis of these tests is questionable. Guidance of deprived children in terms of vocational plans, and college entrance, on the basis of I.Q. tests should be discouraged. In fact, most tests, including personality tests, do not enable us to make accurate appraisals of these children. This is true not only because of the content of the tests themselves, but also because of the relationship between the middle-class examiner and the deprived subject, and the latter's lack of sufficient motivation, practice, and reading ability. The problem of rapport is even greater between a white examiner and a Negro child.

Studies indicate that I.Q. scores of deprived children can be improved dramatically within as little as three days when these factors are controlled and the examiner is trained to understand and work with these youngsters.[1]

The psychological testing program as a whole is not particularly attractive to deprived children. They are troubled by the fact that a good deal of the guidance they receive, apparently based on these tests, takes the form of placement in special classes.

The Davis–Haggard investigators have two fundamental recommendations. One is the development of "culture fair" intelligence tests with questions equally applicable to all groups. There are problems in achieving this policy, however, and until it has been accomplished successfully, the best policy for school personnel would seem to be—teach! Don't use tests to tell you whether the children are teachable; make the assumption that they can learn, and push it to the limit.

Another recommendation, stemming largely from Haggard and the Chicago School, is the need to develop in *all* children the requisite skills and attitudes that directly and indirectly affect test performance. One of the most important of these skills is the ability to *read*.

The teacher can also try to discover the "hidden I.Q.'s" of the deprived children. This can best be done by observing them in games and by noting their contributions in discussing a topic that interests them a good deal, such as popular music or the world series. Role-playing (the acting-out of situations) and physical tasks in general are useful for estimating their potential intelligence. The teacher should be careful not to equate intelligence with speed, verbal facility, or test-taking skill. Even though there are some underprivileged children who are faster and more verbal than others, this does not necessarily mean that those lacking in these attributes are less bright. Of course, games, role-playing, and the like are useful mainly for forming crude evaluations of intelligence in the early stages, before the children

[1] Ernest H. Haggard, "Social-Status and Intelligence," *Genetic Psychology Monographs*, Vol. 49, 1954, pp. 141–186. Also personal communication from Dr. Haggard.

have developed academic skills and motivations. Later on, their actual work will provide a much better barometer of their potential, and standard I.Q. tests may be utilized judiciously. These tests can only be meaningful when the children have sufficient practice, motivation, test-taking skill, reading ability, and a good relationship to the examiner.

Another Style of Thinking

Deprived children are capable of developing abstract, symbolic thinking. They appear to develop this type of thinking in a slower, more indirect fashion; that is, they require more examples before "seeing the point." There is no reason to assume that gifted children have to learn rapidly, although this is the implicit assumption in our culture today. Some individuals take a long time to learn a few basic concepts, but when they finally do so, they may utilize these ideas in a thoughtful, creative fashion. Much more attention needs to be given to the *slow-gifted child*. The underprivileged child has a cognitive style or way of learning that includes a number of features that have unique creative potential: his skill in non-verbal communication (he is not word-bound), his proclivity for persisting along one line (one track creativity), his induction emphasis on many concrete examples, and his colorful free associative feeling for metaphor in language, perhaps best seen in his use of slang. These potentialities, indigenous to his cultural heritage, must be fully explored in any program concerned with developing talent among underprivileged groups.

The New Reader

The general estimate of reading inability among school children is 15 to 20 per cent, while among educationally deprived children the disability estimate is as high as 50 per cent. The significance of reading cannot be overestimated because all too often the deprived child remains retarded in all other subjects due to his inability to read. Junior high school teachers with whom we have spoken insist that they have to spend a large portion of the term teaching reading before they can start serious work on the subject matter of the course they are supposedly giving.

The development of reading ability is particularly important for the slow physical learner, for it is the key to overcoming his academic deficiencies and anti-intellectualism. Perhaps the most effective technique with deprived children is to "externalize" the reading. They have to read about things that they see, feel, and do.

Results of a three-year research program conducted at the University of Michigan indicate that three-fourths of the first grade children who "can't" learn to read may be helped by special attention and instruction. "In the average first grade classroom of thirty pupils, there are eight 'can't' or children who do not make normal reading progress in the early grades. Six of the eight may be helped to overcome their problems," says Donald E. P. Smith, director of the University's Reading Clinic.

There is a great need for readers and materials more attuned to the experiences and problems of deprived groups. The textbooks now used in the school present predominantly middle-class illustrations, rarely concerning themselves with problems or heroes (e.g., Willy Mays) of the disadvantaged.

The problem goes deeper, however, than revising the readers for disadvantaged children. Leacock points out that what is needed is "a more reality-oriented program for all children." She states that:

> A critical look at basic readers from the viewpoint of their discordance with 'lower-class culture,' reveals at a second look a discordance also with what is real experience for most middle-class children. One might ask how typical *are* Dick and Jane, or more important, how meaningful are they and their neat white house in the suburbs to children whose world includes all the blood and thunder, as well as the sophisticated reportage, of television. In what sense do Dick and Jane even reflect middle-class *ideal* patterns in the contemporary world? That such textbook characters help form ideal patterns in the early years is true, but does this not only create a problem for children, when the norms for behavior Dick and Jane express are so far removed from reality? One can even play with the idea of cultural deprivation for middle-class children, since home and school join in building a protective barrier between them and so much of the modern world; and one can wonder what the implications of this protection are for their mental health. Certainly such

readers do not arouse interest in reading, which develops in spite of, not because of, their content.

It would be an exciting idea to have primers which deal more directly with people and events which arouse the emotions of sympathy, curiosity and wonder in children, texts which recognize whimsy as important in the building of values, which accept the adventurous hero as a valid character for children to respond to, which deal with the "child's world" as reaching from home and family to the moon. What contrast to the vapid amiability of Dick and Jane! And how important to have basic readers in which some children live in white houses in suburbs, but many more, equally important as human beings, live in tenements, or apartments, or on farms, in the west, the north, the south, so that all children can read about all others, and, as Americans, get to know their world as it is. Nor, it should be added, is the same purpose served by a mechanical translation of Dicks and Janes to other places and periods in upper-grade readers.[2]

A Specialized Teacher Education Program

Steps should be taken to reorganize teacher education in the colleges, where, by and large, it is predicated on middle-class norms. Courses currently given should be recast, and new courses about the teaching of the educationally deprived should be introduced. Haggard was successful in teaching his examiners how to respond more sensitively to the deprived children they tested.

Future teachers have to understand that the problems encountered in teaching the underprivileged are not due simply to crowded classrooms or poor teachers. These factors play a role, but the important lesson the prospective teacher must assimilate is that teaching deprived children is a special problem requiring special knowledge. In many cases, teachers and administrators lack the basic theory for understanding the problems of the deprived.

There is a real need for a specialized teacher education program directed toward preparing teachers and administrators for working with underprivileged children. This program should be interdisciplinary, enabling education majors to integrate courses

[2] Eleanor Leacock, comment in "Minority Group and Class Status as Related to Social and Personality Factors in Scholastic Achievement," by Martin Deutsch, Monograph No. 2, 1960, published by the Society For Applied Anthropology, New York, pp. 31–32.

in many fields, such as applied anthropology, sociology, political science, economics, and psychology. Education training would thus be greatly broadened as well as intensified. The program should also be urban-centered; that is, concerned with problems of urban migration and redevelopment. It ought to include an intensive understanding of the nature of the city as viewed by the urban sociologist, the housing expert, the student of government, the economist, and so on. The students might be required to select courses from a list such as the following: minority groups, delinquency and criminology, municipal government, social psychology, applied anthropology, urban sociology, Negro history, labor economics, labor history, and industrial psychology. If possible there should be paid internships for selected students who would work in underprivileged communities for one day each week with ministers, social workers, newspaper writers, and other leaders of the community. A special workshop, directed toward integrating the program and discussing the culture of the various minority groups in detail would be crucial for this type of project.

Knowledge and understanding of the deprived cannot come from courses and books alone, although we should not underestimate their value. *Experiences* can be particularly valuable, especially when they are carefully discussed and absorbed. Such experiences might include visiting P.T.A. meetings, community centers, schools or classes where some of the problems have been dealt with successfully, fraternal groups and social clubs. Future teachers should have the opportunity of observing and talking with children from a deprived background who are now doing well in the school. (A special in-service program for school principals would be advisable because of the extremely important roles they play in establishing the atmosphere of the school and in teacher selection.)

The Problem of Teacher Turnover

Because so many teachers refuse jobs at special service schools (in underprivileged areas), and so many leave shortly after having accepted the positions, the problem of teacher preparation and placement is especially acute. Hunter College has developed a promising approach to this problem that has already evidenced some measure of success.[3]

The major aim is "the establishment of a program that would lead to a stable staff in multiproblem schools." Most teacher training programs attempt to prepare student teachers for as many types of schools as possible. The Hunter plan is just the reverse. The student teacher is given special training in the problems of a particular school, in this case a school in an under-privileged neighborhood of Harlem. The student teachers who volunteer, and only volunteers are accepted at this point, "may elect to remain as regular teachers in the school when they complete their student teaching." (At first only a small group volunteered, but as a result of the success of the Program, the number has increased greatly.) The volunteers were prepared to teach in this school by first having them become thoroughly acquainted with the community in which the school is situated. They took trips to the area, spoke to community leaders like the editor of the Negro newspaper *The Amsterdam News*, local ministers of storefront churches, social workers at the Youth Board. They visited a housing project, looked at a typical apartment, sat around in the playground, and talked to the director about the problems many deprived families experience in obtaining an apartment in a public housing project. They also visited the local hospital and talked to the police captain and local political leaders to get their viewpoints about the problems of these children. They were also encouraged to visit the homes of the children and to read the Negro press.

The teachers learned of the hopes and aspirations of the various ethnic groups in the neighborhood. They came to understand why these people were often hostile to the school. Through the development of understanding of the people and their institutions, tendencies toward condescension and snobbery were overcome. The teachers stopped being afraid as mutual respect was built up.

At the school itself, the student teachers spent two weeks observing teachers who have been picked because of their good record with these children. Gradually the student teachers began to work with the classes and then took over completely. Once a

---

[3] Personal communication from Vernon Halprecht of Hunter College, Department of Education.

week all the student teachers had intensive conferences with Dr. Halprecht, the Program's coordinator at Hunter College. They were also placed for one day each in various offices of the school such as the guidance office, the attendance office, the assistant principal's office.

An important feature of the Hunter College Training Program is the "team approach." The student teachers go to the neighborhood together, discuss their teaching experiences together, and are guided as a group by the Hunter staff. The opportunity to share experiences, the mutual reinforcement that eventuates, is a crucial feature of the Program. The teacher no longer feels alone and inadequate, as she so often does in these schools.

When the student teachers graduated and entered the special service school as regular teachers, they did not require special orientation programs for they were completely prepared for the difficulties to be faced and there was no shock or disillusionment. There has been practically no turnover among this initial group and the teachers report considerable satisfaction.[4]

Teacher Continuity and the Multiple Period

High teacher turnover is related to a problem of considerable importance to the underprivileged child; namely, teacher continuity. Deutsch suggests that the "instability of the broken home might be somewhat compensated by children having the same teacher over a longer period of time."[5] The fact that the child changes teachers all the time, together with the fact that he moves so often, contributes to a lack of rootedness in the school.

An experimental program called "Bridge," currently being developed jointly at Queens College and Public School No. 40 in Queens, aims to provide the deprived children with the same teacher over a period of three years. It is quite likely that this increase in teacher continuity will enable the child to develop greater identification with the teacher.

One of the best ways to foster teacher continuity at the junior high school level is the multiple-period class. This provides a

[4] *Ibid.*
[5] Martin Deutsch, "Minority Group and Class Status as Related to Social and Personality Factors in Scholastic Achievement," Monograph No. 2, 1960, published by the Society For Applied Anthropology, p. 28.

better transition from the elementary school where one teacher has the child all day, to the high school single-period system. It is also especially appropriate for the deprived child who needs a great deal of close personal attention. The forty-minute period hardly gives the teacher much of a chance to get to know and work with these children. Also, much more work has to be done during school time, because, in the early stages at least, homework is not as dependably produced. In the multiple-period the children can construct an entire letter. With these children, it is not as though a demonstration lesson can be given on how to write a letter, and then the actual letter be assigned for homework. This will not work. It is far better to have the entire letter constructed from beginning to end in one three-periods-long class. Trips also can be much more profitably arranged in the multiple-period structure. The trip can be discussed both before and afterwards on the very same day.

Teaching Machines and Programmed Learning

There is a great need for increased utilization of teaching machines and programmed, "automated" learning for deprived children, especially in the classes for "slow learners," and in the early stages of transition to the school. Teaching machines can also be used most effectively at the pre-school level.

Special educational programming can be geared to the culture and thinking of the deprived child. Since the child can proceed at his own rate, there is less chance for the development of shame or anxiety on the part of the slow youngster. If a child moves from one school to another he takes his program with him. Moreover, teachers who have great difficulty adapting to the style of the underprivileged child can use the specially designed program as a base.

There are a number of other advantages for the deprived youngster: the "programming automates teaching by breaking information into small, sequential steps that can be exhibited one by one in a machine (or page by page in a book). The program writer is compelled to use the utmost logic and clarity."[6] This step-by-step approach fits in very well with the inductive, careful style of the educationally deprived slow learner.

[6] *Time Magazine*, March 24, 1961, p. 36.

"Questioning the student at each step, riveting his attention and rewarding him—immediately and continually with the satisfaction of being right,"[7] is again especially attuned for the unconfident learner who, in the early stages at least, needs "fast reinforcement."

The test-taking deficiencies of the underprivileged can also be overcome through the programming, as the test format is utilized without the disturbing competitive overtones of most school tests. The individual is striving for mastery of the program at his own pace; he is not competing directly against other children.

Lastly, the mechanical, gadgety, game-like character of automated learning is likely to have special appeal for the physically oriented, underprivileged youth.

A Peace Corps For the Deprived

Much fanfare is being given to the Peace Corps, in which young people serve as diplomatic representatives and technical aids in foreign lands. This is a splendid idea, but one which is not likely to favor the educationally deprived youngster. What the government can do for the deprived lies largely in the field of education, especially higher education. During World War II, the ASTP (Army Specialized Training Program) sent to college many underprivileged young men who would never otherwise have had this opportunity. This was a successful program, and with the current expansion of military functions there is no reason why it could not be resurrected. The army might also increase its vocational training program at the less advanced, non-college level, as this is particularly attractive to disadvantaged youths who frequently enlist to learn a skill for which they could not afford to pay in civilian life. Few things are more effective in combating delinquency than job preparation and education with an eye to the future. The aimlessness which characterizes so many young people could, to some degree, be counteracted by a developed educational program. This, of course, need not take place in the military services alone. An expanded government scholarship aid program for the needy would play a tremendous role also.

[7] *Ibid.*

Research Agenda

The need for intensive research concerning the disadvantaged child is considerable. We need to know much more about the various dimensions of his mental style. We need better instruments to uncover his hidden intelligence. We need new and more appropriate personality tests to assess his character. (The Rorschach and the Thematic Apperception Test are, in the main, unsuitable for educationally deprived individuals. There is a need for cartoon-like tests such as the Rosenzweig Frustration Test, and simple picture selection instruments such as the Szondi (not demanding verbal story telling as in the T.A.T.).[8] We need more information on why some of the siblings of poor learners often do well in school. (The Institute for Developmental Studies is now investigating this problem.)

There is a great need for centralization of research about the teaching of the deprived. On the simplest level, teachers with a demonstrated flair for successful instruction of deprived children should be observed and their practices analyzed. On a more ambitious level, experimentation in teaching practices should be set in motion.

A basic bibliography on the educationally deprived should be provided for in-service training programs as well as for college and graduate school programs.

Suggestion Survey

Let us briefly list a series of suggestions that have been made in this book and elsewhere, and include also a survey of practices that are in the early stages of development throughout the country:

——The employment of more psychologists, teachers, and social workers who themselves come from a deprived background would be of great aid, because these people have experienced this life from the "inside." The same suggestion holds true in terms of hiring more Negro psychologists and teachers. However, sometimes these individuals are removed from the groups of their origin, and their understanding cannot be counted on in

[8] See Frank Riessman and S. M. Miller, "Social Class and Projective Techniques," *Journal of Projective Techniques*, Vol. 22, 1958, pp. 432–439.

a mechanical fashion. Nevertheless, they often have valuable information and understanding, and their very presence in the school is generally responded to positively by the children and parents.

——Psychotherapeutic methods that stress authority, directiveness, the physical aspect, the group and the family, action rather than talk alone (e.g., role-playing), are likely to be far more successful than introspective depth orientations. The educationally deprived person in therapy is more likely to see his problems as externally- (rather than internally-) caused, to want a doctor's prescription, to prefer action to words, and to want his "symptoms" cured rather than to submit to a complete overhauling of his personality.

——The deprived are not especially fond of progressive methods —the "new program." They feel it is unstructured, does not stress learning sufficiently, underestimates discipline and the authority of the teacher. Consequently, if a teacher wishes to employ a "progressive" approach, some emendation of it would seem necessary. The one feature of progressive education that is congenial to deprived children is related to "learning by doing." This fits in with their physical approach to learning. It is possible that this feature has not been responded to as positively as might be expected because it is embedded in the larger progressive context which is unappealing to the deprived. A basic traditional structure, combined with an emphasis on physical learning, would probably be most effective.

——School re-zoning should be intensively planned in order to remove the segregated school patterns that have emerged. School districting, which tends to segregate youths from different social strata, lessens the educational aspirations of underprivileged youngsters.

——The labor movement should be more fully involved in cooperating with the schools in the planning and the carrying-through of special educational programs for the disadvantaged.

——Five- and perhaps six-year college programs should be anticipated and organized for slow learners who have basic abilities, but require more time because of their work styles.

——Special rooms should be set aside in the school so that children who have difficulty working at home, because of noise and non-educational TV, can work in a quiet atmosphere. The trend toward the increased use of the school after hours by community groups, English classes, special cooking classes, etc., should spread rapidly. This will help to break down the separation of the school and the underprivileged community.

The following quotations are taken from the "Great Cities School Improvement Studies:"[9]

——"An extended school day and school week (to include field trips to civic, recreational, industrial, and other centers of interest, as well as reading clinics, opportunities for recreational reading in the school library, small group academic coaching, and small group guidance) . . . will improve the achievement of the culturally deprived in reading and arithmetic, will improve their motivation, and decrease the number who drop out of school before high school graduation."

——"A flexible, non-graded grouping of children in the elementary school will permit individuals to complete, for example, a given three-year block of work in four years or in two years, will reduce discouragement on the part of slower children, and will make it possible for the more able to accelerate and/or enrich their learning."

——"The organization of centers or classes to provide a special program for the culturally deprived child who is of high school age but has not completed the elementary school program will result in fewer failures, a decreased drop-out rate, improved social behavior patterns, better motivation for learning, and better terminal programs for children who will not continue their formal education."

——Smaller classes (lower student–teacher ratios) are imperative for disadvantaged children but,

"Varying the sizes of classes within the school day (so that the particular talents of some teachers are brought to large groups of children, and at the same time other teachers, who may have talents for working with the culturally deprived in small groups or as individuals, are freed for work of this type) will improve reading and arithmetic skills, heighten appreciation of music or literature because of the response of a large group to expert interpretation, utilize space in buildings not now being used regularly (auditoriums, very small rooms)."

——"An organization in which the length of the periods in the

[9] Ford Foundation Project, mimeographed, 1960.

school day is altered to give the culturally deprived child some short periods of instruction in small groups in skill areas and longer periods of integrated unit activity will improve reading and arithmetic skills, establish the close, stabilizing relationship with an adult . . . and help the child to see the relationship among the subject areas."

——Greater use of "master" (or "consulting") teachers is urged. "During the period that the use of large numbers of inexperienced teachers is necessary, the work of these teachers can be improved and geared to the specific needs of the culturally deprived child through the guidance of expert teachers assigned to work on an in-service, in-the-classroom basis." An increased effort should be made to encourage excellent teachers to become "master" teachers rather than school administrators.

——Increased use of non-professional personnel (team mothers, fathers, grandmothers) "for such purposes as vision and hearing screening, escorting pupils on field trips, operating projectors and other equipment will release professional personnel for teaching purposes and improve the academic achievement of the culturally deprived as well as meet many of their other needs." (These people are receiving salaries in various schools throughout the country.)

The following suggestions were made by Patricia Sexton:[10]

——"Efforts should be made to encourage more men, of the type boys can readily identify with, to enter teaching."

——"Teachers with some zeal for teaching lower-income students should be encouraged to come into the profession."

——"The distribution of qualified teachers should be equalized, or inequalities compensated for. Pay teachers more in schools where it is difficult to get teachers, or provide other rewards; teachers in these schools should be especially singled out for notice and attention."

——Instructional facilities should also be equalized, and libraries in deprived neighborhoods should be kept open as many days per week as they are in non-deprived neighborhoods.

——More college scholarships should be provided for low income students, as well as financial aid while going to high school. Free books should be provided.

[10] Patricia Sexton, *Education and Income*, (New York: The Viking Press, Inc., 1961), pp. 259, 264–265, 267–268, 271–272, 275.

——"All segregated groupings and curriculums, except those of a very temporary nature, should be eliminated. A special preparatory class might be given in the last year of high school for those who plan to attend college. Segregation in the early grades is particularly dangerous and unfair."

——"The present, highly competitive, system of marks, exams, and comparisons of all sorts should be replaced by other types of incentives to learning. If there is to be competition, emphasis should be on group, rather than on individual, competition. Marks and grades hurt more than they help; they discourage students from studying 'hard' subjects or taking good but tough teachers; they discourage really independent and critical thinking, since the teacher who marks you cannot be questioned or challenged too much; and they tend to make 'good' students conformists and 'bad' students rebellious."

——"Group projects and group planning are excellent learning devices. Yet they are hard to use in the typical classroom because of the commotion and discipline problems that can result in an overcrowded classroom. Adjustments should be made in room equipment, room size, and class size to make such projects easier to handle. Groups, working with a purpose, can often themselves discipline individual members without teacher interference."

——"The dead weight of meaningless dates and data should be removed from the curriculum and replaced with learning activities and knowledge that will be purposeful, meaningful, and intellectually stimulating. Education should begin with an inquiry into needs. What does the child *need* to know? What does society *need* him to know—now, and in the future? Not, what have we been teaching him for the past half-century? Not, what is in the textbook used in the course? Not, what is in *any* text, or *any* book, necessarily? Not even, what will colleges require him to know?—for they too can be giant storage bins for dead knowledge."

——"There should be more work-study programs. At the same time, purely vocational training should be de-emphasized in the schools, since this training often becomes obsolete before it can be used; also, special 'trade' and 'vocational' schools should be discontinued, unless the vocational curriculum is liberal in approach and broad in character. Such schools are often used as dumping grounds for students who are not wanted elsewhere, and often little more than custodial care is provided in them. Where more is provided, the skills taught are frequently of too perishable a nature."

——"As for extra-curricular activities, there should be more emphasis on sports, and recreational and cultural activities that will involve all students rather than a select few. The sports program, especially, should not be so exclusive as it is now; all boys who want to play should be put on teams."

——"The library should be a focal point of the school, attractive, easy to use, accessible to students at all times, and continuing instruction should be given in library use for research and general reading purposes."

——"As part of the English program, continuing instruction should also be given in reading, study, and homework skills, with more direct attention to an unexplainably neglected skill—concentration, a prerequisite for all productive mental activity and one that bothers lower-status students more than others, as study has shown."

——Effort must be made to overcome the highly inappropriate teaching of grammar and language usage.

> . . . while grammar exercises seem designed to help no one, usage exercises seem designed to help only those students (usually from middle- and upper-income groups) who commit minor infractions of the rules. So it is that continuing references are made in texts to misplaced commas, the forms of 'lie' and 'lay,' the use of 'who' and 'whom,' dangling participles, etc., with a sprinkling of the grosser errors committed by lower-income students.
>
> As a basic beginning, some effort should be made to discover the exact nature of the language problem in various student groups—Negro, Southern white, Polish, Italian . . . etc.—so that instruction could be tailor-made to their groups, and individual needs. Perhaps this would mean abandoning the grammar text completely in favor of special short-form exercises adapted to real student problems.

This book has attempted to outline an approach to the educationally deprived child. I have used phrases such as "understand

and respect" the culture, "begin with the interests of the under-privileged," and so on. In conclusion, let me state briefly the three levels that are involved in this approach:

1. At the simplest level, the approach requires a recognition of the educational deficiencies that result from the life conditions of the underprivileged. Here would be included the confusion and ambivalence about education, the limited reading ability, the fear of failure, the inadequate test-taking skills, and lack of school know-how.

2. At the next level the approach calls attention to the fact that the underprivileged have specific interests, like science, auto-mobiles, sports, and that these interests can be used as "openers" for developing educational understanding. Under this heading, too, would be included role-playing and other physical and visual techniques. It is a common mistake for the teacher to believe that she need only *recognize* these interests in order to make contact with the child. She may find any genuine appreciation of these "low level" interests impossible for her. *If the teacher cannot in any way appreciate the interests of the deprived, it will be difficult for her to see any possible continuity between these interests and advanced education;* consequently, the recognition of dif-ferences in background, while it may lead to a pleasanter class-room atmosphere, does not necessarily produce real educational progress.

3. The highest level is what we call the "cultural approach," by which we mean a genuine respect for the efforts of the de-prived in coping with difficult life conditions. Many of the in-stitutions and values that characterize the life of disadvantaged groups have arisen from these efforts. While some of these tradi-tions have proven more effective than others, many of them, it seems to us, deserve some measure of respect. Under this heading we would include the extended family, the cooperative and equalitarian traditions, the anger and alienation, the desire for structure, the informality, and humor.

Finally, I would like to reaffirm that understanding traditions does not require that we be uncritical of them. This is particularly pertinent with regard to the anti-intellectualism and narrow prac-ticality of the deprived. In the context of basic respect and ap-proval, criticism can be most welcome.

BIBLIOGRAPHY

Berger, Bennett, *Working Class Suburb*, Berkeley: University of California Press, 1960.

Bernstein, Basil, "A Public Language: Some Sociological Implications of a Linguistic Form," *British Journal of Sociology*, December, 1959, pp. 311–327.

Bettelheim, Bruno, "Sputnik and Segregation," *Commentary*, October, 1958, pp. 332–339.

Bronfenbrenner, Urie, "Socialization and Social Class through Time and Space," in E. E. Maccoby, T. M. Newcomb, and R. L. Hartley, eds., *Readings in Social Psychology*, New York: Henry Holt, 1958, pp. 400–425.

Centers, Richard, *The Psychology of Social Classes*, Princeton: Princeton University Press, 1949.

Chinoy, Ely, *American Workers and Their Dreams*, New York: Doubleday, 1955.

Cohen, Albert, *Delinquent Boys: The Culture of the Gang*, Glencoe: The Free Press, 1955.

Davidson, Helen, and Lang, Gerhard, "Children's Perceptions of Their Teachers' Feelings Toward Them Related to Self-Perception, School Achievement and Behavior," *Journal of Experimental Education*, December, 1960, pp. 107–118.

Davidson, Helen, Riessman, Frank, and Meyers, Edna, "Personality Characteristics Attributed to Various Occupational Groups," *Journal of Social Psychology*, 1962 (in press).

Davis, Allison, *Social Class Influences Upon Learning*, Cambridge: Harvard University Press, 1948.

Davis, Allison, and Havighurst, Robert J., "Social Class and Color Differences in Child Rearing," *American Sociological Review*, April, 1953, pp. 142–149.

Deutsch, Martin, "Minority Groups and Class Status as Related to Social and Personality Factors in Scholastic Achievement," Monograph published by Society For Applied Anthropology, New York, 1960.

Dotson, Floyd, "Patterns of Voluntary Association Among Urban

Working Class Families," *American Sociological Review*, October, 1951, pp. 687–693.

Douvan, Elizabeth, "Social Status and Success Striving," *Journal of Abnormal and Social Psychology*, March, 1956, pp. 219–223.

Duvall, Evelyn Millis, "Conceptions of Parenthood," *American Journal of Sociology*, November, 1946, pp. 193–203.

Eells, Kenneth, *et al.*, *Intelligence and Cultural Differences*, Chicago: University of Chicago Press, 1951.

Goodman, Paul, *Growing Up Absurd*, New York: Random House, 1960.

Haggard, Ernest A., "Techniques for the Development of Unbiased Tests," *1952 Invitational Conference on Testing Problems*.

——, "Social Status and Intelligence," *Genetic Psychology Monograph*, No. 49, 1954, pp. 141–186.

Hollingshead, A. B., and Redlich, Frederick C., *Social Class and Mental Illness*, New York: John Wiley & Sons, Inc., 1958.

Hyman, Herbert H., "The Values Systems of Different Classes: A Social Psychological Contribution to the Analysis of Stratification," in Bendix, Reinhard, and Lipset, Seymour M., *Class, Status, and Power*, Glencoe: The Free Press, 1953, pp. 426–442.

Kahl, Joseph A., *The American Class Structure*, New York: Rinehart, 1959.

Kinsey, Alfred C., *et al.*, *Sexual Behavior in the Human Male*, Philadelphia: Saunders, 1948.

Knupfer, Genevieve, "Portrait of the Underdog," in Bendix, Reinhard, and Lipset, Seymour M., *Class, Status, and Power*, Glencoe: The Free Press, 1953, pp. 255–263.

Kohn, Melvin L., "Social Class and the Exercise of Parental Authority," *American Sociological Review*, June, 1959, pp. 364–365.

Lipset, Seymour M., *Political Man: The Social Bases of Politics*, New York: Doubleday, 1960, Chapter IV.

Maccoby, Eleanor E., *et al.*, "Methods of Child Rearing in Two Social Classes," in Martin, William E., and Stendler, Celia B., *Readings in Child Development*, New York: Harcourt, Brace & Company, 1954.

Miller, S. M., and Riessman, Frank, "The Working Class Subculture: A New View," *Social Problems*, Summer, 1961, pp. 86–97.

——, "Are Workers Middle Class?" *Dissent*, Winter, 1961.

——, "Working-Class Authoritarianism: A Critique of Lipset," *British Journal of Sociology*, September, 1961.

Miller, Daniel R., and Swanson, Guy E., *Inner Conflict and Defense*, New York: Henry Holt, 1960.

Morse, Arthur D., *Schools of Tomorrow—Today*, New York: Doubleday, 1960.

Mulligan, Raymond A., "Socio-Economic Background and College Enrollment," *American Sociological Review*, April, 1951, pp. 188–196.

Murray, Walter, "Some Major Assumptions Underlying the Development of Intelligence Tests," Unpublished, 1960.

Rainwater, Lee, *And The Poor Get Children*, Chicago: Quadrangle Books, Inc., 1961.

Riessman, Frank, *Workers' Attitudes Towards Participation and Leadership*, Unpublished Ph.D. dissertation, Columbia University, 1955.

Riessman, Frank, and Miller, S. M., "Participation, Culture and Personality," *Journal of Social Issues*, Winter, 1949.

——, "Social Class and Projective Techniques," *Journal of Projective Techniques*, November, 1958, pp. 432–439.

Rodman, Hyman, "On Understanding Lower-Class Behavior," *Social and Economics Studies*, December, 1959, pp. 441–450.

Schneider, Louis, and Lysgaard, Sverre, "The Deferred Gratification Pattern: A Preliminary Study," *American Sociological Review*, April, 1953, pp. 142–149.

Sears, Robert R., *et al.*, *Patterns of Child Rearing*, Evanston: Row, Peterson & Company, 1957.

Sexton, Patricia, *Education and Income*, New York: The Viking Press, Inc., 1961.

Siller, Jerome, "Socio-economic Status and Conceptual Thinking," *Journal of Abnormal and Social Psychology*, November, 1957, pp. 365–371.

Useem, John, Tangent, Pierre, and Useem, Ruth, "Stratification in a Prairie Town," *American Sociological Review*, June, 1942, pp. 331–342.

Vincent, Clark E., "The Unwed Mother and Sampling Bias," *American Sociological Review*, October, 1954, pp. 562–567.

Walker, Charles R., *Steeltown*, New York: Harper & Brothers, 1950.

Weaver, Robert C., "Human Values of Urban Life," *Proceedings of the Academy of Political Science*, May, 1960, pp. 33–41.

Whyte, William F., *Street Corner Society*, Chicago: University of Chicago Press, 1943.

Wilson, Allen B., "Class Segregation and Aspirations of Youth," *American Sociological Review*, December, 1959, pp. 836–845.

INDEX